Praise for *There is Another Way*

This is an important collection of essays that explore alternative ways forward for education. The contributions are thoughtful, committed, passionate, idealistic and, ultimately, radical. They offer moral, pragmatic and practical alternative perspectives and share a deep and abiding concern for the learning and development of children as the core focus of any education system. The range of topics covered provides a powerful resource for a fundamental critique of existing policies and taken together they offer a holistic view of an alternative future. Collectively the chapters 'speak truth to power' and will stimulate thinking, debate and reflection about the future course of education.

John West-Burnham, Professor of Educational Leadership,
St Mary's University College

At one point in *There is Another Way*, Nina Jackson – discussing mental health issues – writes, 'Reassure the person that with help and support they can get through the emotional trauma they are experiencing.' That line could be the strapline for this book, a book which reassures those of us who have, even for a second, begun to think that what we have been doing in our teaching careers for years was wrong. I, for one, have felt huge emotional trauma when things I thought were important in a learning community – relationships, humanity and love – have been trumped by political diktat, distrust and textbooks.

There is a host of great educators writing here. The Real David Cameron stands up for experience over research. Bethan Stracy-Burbridge articulates beautifully the benefits of art therapy and how every interaction we have with a child *matters*. Professor Paul Clarke poses a question which gets to the nub of why we are here and how can we remain part of planet earth. Rachel Jones reminds us that there is no 'what works' rulebook. And if you were thinking of doing away with books in this digital age, you'd better read Sarah Pavey's essay on why libraries are more important than ever! This is no backward-looking tome, however: Mark

Anderson and Simon Pridham give us sparkling insights into how new technologies can shape learning in the future.

In his signature essay Ian Gilbert, the driving force behind *There is Another Way*, urges us all, especially our students, to ask the eternal question of anything and anyone – why? It is the question which we should be asking of education policymakers of all political hues. If this book does just one thing it will help those in education whose beliefs have been eroded by over-confident politicians over the last decade to reassert an educational values-system which puts humanity back into the centre of the ring. With *There is Another Way* none of us need to be emotionally traumatised any longer.

John Tomsett, Head Teacher, Huntington School

The years of experience the writers combine to produce this book mean that there is something for every reader. The authors bring professional wisdom, insight, knowledge and sense to address the confusion and clamour of the present climate. At the heart of the book is a shared concern for the best in schools and the greatest impact on children's futures. The book is a joy to read, a real treasure trove of thinking and practice; there is a jewel for everyone.

Mick Waters, Professor of Education, Wolverhampton University

It is easy to find books encouraging you to change your way of teaching (without showing you any clues). It is more difficult to discover one, written by real teachers, not only saying that another way is possible, but also indicating where that way is. A pleasure to read this inspirational and practical book which moves the reader into a future that he knows he can make real: the future of an education with the children as its only concern.

Juan Carlos García García, Pedagogical, Pastoral and Innovation Department,
Escuelas Católicas de Madrid

I got a huge amount out of this wide-ranging book. I think others will too. It's full of wisdom and great insight. *There is Another Way* is a compilation of the thoughts of some of our top thinkers on pedagogy, politics, research, curriculum, coaching, mental health, restorative practice, behaviour and values. It starts with a terrific list of aspirations for all of us in education.

It's well worth getting a copy. It will refresh your thinking.

Mary Myatt, adviser and inspector

I love this book. Sequels aren't always a good idea, but the Second Big Book of Independent Thinking is a really good idea. It exudes optimism at a time when there isn't always enough optimism, laughter or fun in our schools. Yet it isn't afraid to challenge us, to be gritty, to urge us to be bolder in what we value and how we teach. At a time when there's too much dashing after quick-fixes in schools, the authors of *There is Another Way* take us back to first principles about learning, the nature of schools and why many of us decided to become teachers in the first place. It's a terrific and feisty read, an indispensable inoculation against the educational gloom that can too easily infect us.

Geoff Barton, Head Teacher, King Edward VI School

My belief that 'there is another way' is the reason I get out of bed in the morning. The fact that so many others have captured all the feelings I have in my heart about education gives me the courage to be brave and clearer in my own mind about providing the right balance between knowledge, skills, values and behaviours. When I finished the book, I realised this was the start of the process, not the end. I want to do something, no matter how small, to make a commitment to change, to make a difference.

David Hanson, Chief Executive, IAPS

There is Another Way

The Second Big Book of Independent Thinking

Ian Gilbert

with Mark Anderson, Lisa Jane Ashes, Phil Beadle, Jackie Beere,
David Cameron (The Real David Cameron), Paul Clarke, Tait Coles, Mark Creasy,
Mark Finnis, Dave Harris, Crista Hazell, Martin Illingworth, Nina Jackson,
Rachel Jones, Gill Kelly, Debra Kidd, Jonathan Lear, Trisha Lee, Roy Leighton,
Matthew McFall, Sarah Pavey, Simon Pridham, Jim Roberson, Hywel Roberts,
Martin Robinson, Bethan Stracy-Burbridge, Dave Whitaker and Phil Wood

Independent Thinking Press

First published by

Independent Thinking Press

Crown Buildings, Bancyfelin, Carmarthen, Wales, SA33 5ND, UK

www.independentthinkingpress.com

Independent Thinking Press is an imprint of Crown House Publishing Ltd.

Independent Thinking Press has no responsibility for the persistence or accuracy of URLs for external or third-party websites referred to in this publication, and does not guarantee that any content on such websites is, or will remain, accurate or appropriate.

Cover illustration by Tania Willis www.taniawillis.com

British Library Cataloguing-in-Publication Data

A catalogue entry for this book is available from the British Library.

Print ISBN 978-178135236-6
Mobi ISBN 978-178135237-3
ePub ISBN 978-1781352380-1
ePDF ISBN 978-178135239-7

Printed and bound in the UK by
TJ International, Padstow, Cornwall

To Sue and Paul
For starting something – thank you

All proceeds from this book go to our work supporting
educational endeavours across the Global Educational Village.

Contents

There is Another Way

1. Insist that your children look 'beneath the surface' and are given the space, encouragement and skills to think for themselves.

2. Take a fresh look at how you organise your curriculum and trust children to respond well when you really stretch them with genuinely authentic learning.

3. See your library as so much more than a room full of books and engage your librarian as an 'information professional' right at the heart of what schools are about.

4. Understand – and help your children understand – that learning is never a straight line and that getting it wrong is an integral step along the way to getting it right.

5. Remember to value children more than data, that children value people more than worksheets, that the best teachers are learners too and that your job is a part of your life, not the other way round.

6. Remember that your school – and its community – are unique. Simply repeating a formula used elsewhere denies all involved the chance to create something special.

7. Engage in educational research to best understand the power of educational research. But know its limitations too.

8. Look for links between subject areas that will bring the curriculum to life and make it a purposeful experience for all learners and not just 'because it's in the exam'.

9. Look beyond their behaviour to the circumstances behind their behaviour and ensure you don't simply rely on simplistic 'sanction and reward' approaches.

10. Challenge everything – superiors, job titles, systems, everything that you feel is getting in the way of all children achieving what they are truly capable of.

11. Value every child in your class relentlessly and regardlessly in both word and deed and remember the extent to which little things can make a lasting difference.

12. Understand the power of wonder to help engage young people and motivate them to learn, then build in opportunities to discover wondrous things across the school.

13. Keep a watchful eye out for the unintended consequences of school improvement measures and always remember that schools are endlessly complex systems.

14. Look beyond what that young person is now to what they could become, with your help, and remember that your influence will reach further than you will ever know.

15. Use technology in learning to enhance great pedagogy not replace it. The skill, for you and them, is to start where you are comfortable, then reach just beyond that.

16. Think carefully about the nature of 'progress' in your school and be aware of what you are losing as well as what you are gaining. Especially when it comes to values.

17. Encourage young people to stand for something, to connect with their community and then to act on what needs changing. And support them all the way.

18. Never confuse research with politics and always entertain new ideas without losing sight of your values, your experience and your common sense – then act accordingly.

19. Use story to tap into children's imagination, to engage them, to help them remember what you've taught and as a starting point for many aspects of the curriculum.

20. Grasp the fact that the world we are educating our children in and for is unsustainable. Take your class outside and reconnect education with something bigger.

21. Mental illness is abundantly evident in – and often provoked by – life in school. Learn about it, know what to do about it and then do what is needed, every time.

22. Plan lessons for your children, in your classroom, in your school, in your community and that are 'worth behaving for'. Use their engagement to reflect on your efficacy.

23. Be aware whose interests are served by the curriculum you teach and the systems of control you employ. Knowledge may well be power but genuine education is about freedom.

24. Focus on relationships more than you focus on behaviour. Focus on values more than you focus on control. Look at your behaviour as much as you look at theirs.

25. Develop your practice in various ways and on an ongoing basis using the many tools available to you these days, with coaching right at the heart of the process.

26. Use technology to make your school credible and their learning relevant but integrate it with your development plan and the needs of the wider community.

27. Make things harder for children, not easier, by using curiosity and novelty as powerful tools to engage young people in their own learning.

28. Seek to combine the curriculum with the reality of their own lives and then plan lessons where moments occur which you cannot plan for.

29. Understand how a young person's actions can be the outer representation of their feelings and the power you have, as a caring adult, to influence both for the better.

Tell us what you think – learn@independentthinking.co.uk

www.independentthinking.com

List of Contributors

Mark Anderson is the man people turn to as the 'ICT Evangelist' to answer all their ICT queries. However, the secret to making digital learning work lies with what is going on in students' heads, not the hardware in their hands. Mark's work shows how we need to create learning environments where we get that right first.

Lisa Jane Ashes is a teacher, trainer, award-winning blogger and the creator of the Manglish concept that links maths and English and develops them together across the curriculum. She sees many flaws in the way schools are organised and has shown that when you break that model you can help them work better.

Phil Beadle is an award-winning teacher, author and columnist with multiple television appearances to his name. He is living proof that sometimes you get the best results for young people by ripping up the rule book and going your own way. The trouble that acting like this gets you into is just something you have to deal with.

Jackie Beere OBE is a vastly experienced school leader, teacher, trainer, coach, writer and editor who has worked at every level from classroom assistant to head teacher and beyond. Drawing on her experience with mindsets, neuro-linguistic programming, skills-based learning and more, she knows how to get the best out of all members of a school community.

David Cameron (known as The Real David Cameron) is an adviser and speaker as well as what can be described as a very active educational activist. He is passionate about education being at the heart of the community and equally passionate that such an education should, in turn, have creativity – and all that this entails – at its heart.

Professor Paul Clarke is a highly regarded and published educator whose experience has seen him advise governments on both educational and ecological matters worldwide. Through his work across the globe, he sees the challenges we are facing and the crucial role education should and must play in helping us to survive.

Tait Coles is the man behind *Punk Learning: Never Mind the Inspectors*. A teacher and SLT member in the north of England, he sees at first hand the way in which the current system disenfranchises large numbers of young people, and how this will come back and haunt us all. He is on a mission to do something about it.

Mark Creasy has worked in all sectors and across all phases of the education system and refuses to accept that lessons have to look like they normally do. His first book, *Unhomework*, examined the broken model of traditional homework and turned it on its head.

Mark Finnis is in demand in organisations nationwide for his powerful work on restorative approaches. For schools, this means that discipline is not something imposed on children, enforced by adults. Instead, the whole area of behaviour is a collaborative, constructed and formative process where everyone can win.

Ian Gilbert is an award-winning author, editor, speaker and innovator and the man who set up Independent Thinking over 20 years ago. In recent years he has become increasingly vexed by the way the education system not only fails to make the world better but actually serves to keep it screwed up.

Dave Harris is a school leader and trainer and the author of *Brave Heads*. His many years leading schools in challenging circumstances have proven to him how important it is for a school leader to think for himself or herself, to work with the whole community and to see a picture well beyond next year's exam results.

Crista Hazell is a teacher of young people first and foremost, and of modern foreign languages second to that. At a time when education has become a numbers game and 'student engagement' a soft option after behavioural sanctions and systems, Crista shows that relentless optimism in young people pays huge dividends.

Martin Illingworth is a university-based teacher trainer, writer, speaker and experienced educator who sees at close up the hypocrisy and folly of so much of what teachers are currently being asked to do. For him, education is not so much a system but a series of moments that last long after the test results have been forgotten.

Nina Jackson has seen first hand the dangers of focusing on academic achievement at the expense of well-being and emotional health. Mental health problems are on the increase in schools – among staff as well as children – and this is an issue we must confront not only as institutions but also as caring individuals.

Rachel Jones is a highly creative teacher with experience across various sectors and phases of the education system. Wisdom comes from experience and experience comes from being brave, trying new things, keeping your eyes open and not doing everything they tell you to.

Gill Kelly is a school leader, speaker and writer who has experienced the complexities of inner-city educational leadership. She knows that genuine education happens when we lift our sights above the paperwork and target chasing and give students a real voice about things that actually matter.

Dr Debra Kidd is a teacher, lecturer, speaker and writer working across all phases of the education system. She draws on her experience in the UK and abroad to be a vocal and persistent thorn in the side of the advocates of a more 'traditional' approach to teaching, one that fails to see the child in the room.

Jonathan Lear is primary school deputy head, writer, speaker and incredible teacher who brings the learning alive for children from challenging inner-city backgrounds. Teaching children facts doesn't make them learners which is why his classroom is a place of discovery, excitement, curiosity and fantasy. And learning.

Trisha Lee is a teacher and writer with her roots very much in theatre. Learning for her is an active, engaging, child-centred process that is stimulated by fantasy and works best, even for traditional subjects such as maths and science, when the teacher is guided by the wonderful fantasies children construct – when we let them.

Roy Leighton is a trainer, speaker, writer and coach with experience both across schools and in the business world. His work shows that learning is not something measured in boxes and straight lines but is a richly complex process done by children, not to them. It is all the more magical because of it.

Dr Matthew McFall is the world's first school-based 'Agent of Wonder' whose (most recent) doctoral thesis explored the powerful role of curiosity and wonder in the learning process. He is the author of *A Cabinet of Curiosities* and is in demand as schools begin to understand that, where threats fail, curiosity can prevail.

Sarah Pavey is a school librarian who is gaining a national reputation for showing schools that a library is a whole lot more than a room full of books. In fact, it might not even be a room at all. The Information Age desperately needs expert guides and modern librarians can do this better than anyone.

Simon Pridham is an award-winning school leader, trainer and writer who shows that learning technologies can transform the lives of some of our most needy young people – but only when done in an inclusive, community-minded way that balances the right technology with the right curriculum and the right pedagogy.

Jim Roberson is the self-styled 'Discipline Coach' and author of the book of the same name. A former professional American football player, Jim draws on his experience in sport, of growing up in the US and of teaching and working with challenging young people in the UK to show how we are more than just teachers, if we let ourselves be.

Hywel Roberts is the man behind the best-selling book *Oops!* He knows full well that you get the most out of young people – and their teachers – not by coercion but by hooking them in with engaging, stimulating and absorbing learning opportunities during which they behave, join in, cooperate and learn, despite themselves.

Martin Robinson is a teacher, speaker and writer whose first book, *Trivium 21c*, has won plaudits from across the educational landscape. Martin argues with eloquence and intelligence that school reform – and educational reform as a whole – needs to consider lessons from the past before any more damage is done.

Bethan Stracy-Burbridge is a leading art therapist and trainer. Her work shows that you cannot successfully educate children unless you are successfully addressing the issues they carry with them, issues whose origins may well be outside of school but that impact on their schooling in serious and significant ways.

Dave Whitaker is a head teacher of an emotional and behavioural difficulties special school, who also oversees a number of pupil referral units and other interventions to help young people. Rather than employing a deficit model, Dave shows that you get the best out of troubled young people by treating them with care, respect and unconditional positive regard.

Dr Phil Wood is an experienced university-based academic, trainer, researcher and writer. He has the intelligence, understanding and wisdom to see through the rhetoric and help teachers stay focused on the real challenges and complexities involved in educating young people – and themselves.

As the indomitable Margaret Thatcher once remarked about neoliberal globalisation, 'There is no alternative' … Was she right?

Not at all.

James H. Mittelman,
Whither Globalization? The Vortex of Knowledge and Ideology (2004)

An equitable approach to pedagogy demands an education system concerned with the development of human capabilities and knowledges of the broadest kind, not one driven by the goal of global economic competitiveness. It requires a system architecture designed to promote learning for all, not one designed to regulate achievement of narrow educational goals and to produce a functioning market for educational providers.

Ruth Lupton and Amelia Hempel-Jorgensen, 'The Importance of Teaching:
Pedagogical Constraints and Possibilities in Working-Class Schools' (2012)

Lee: I always thought it was a mistake at school that you had a lesson called 'History' but not 'Future'.

Lucy: Maybe because at your school the teachers felt you didn't have a future.

Not Going Out, Series 6, Episode 6

Introduction

In 1993 Ian Gilbert set up Independent Thinking to 'change young people's lives by changing the way they think – and so to change the world'.

Since then, joined by some of the UK's leading educational thinkers and innovative practitioners, Independent Thinking has worked in thousands of schools with hundreds of thousands of young people, teachers, leaders, parents and others across the UK and around the world.

Our message has always been one of hope, liberation and respect, putting children at the centre of the educational process with learning something they do, not that is done to them. And, more important than the outcome, it is the process that children go through – and grow through – that is the mark of a great education.

Over two decades, we have seen the educational pendulum swing back and forth but we, like so many great teachers, have striven to remain true to our principles. We exist to make a difference not to make a profit. We work like a family. We do what we can to help anyone who asks. We play nicely. We have a laugh while we're doing it because, as we have said repeatedly, education is too important to be taken seriously.

In 2006, through our friends at Crown House Publishing, we published the first *Big Book of Independent Thinking*, our first foray into putting our voices in print. Since then we have written countless books and the Independent Thinking Press has won awards for pushing the boundaries of what educational publishing should look and feel like.

In 2015 we published our second *Big Book,* at a time when the education we believe in and the education system we feel strongly about are under attack more than ever. There are strong voices across social media, in schools and in power telling teachers and school leaders that 'this is the way to do it', reminiscent of Margaret Thatcher's famous TINA – There Is No Alternative – approach. Yet the way being advocated is a way that runs contrary to what many in the profession believe in.

This book is our message to them – and to teachers everywhere – that no matter what we are told, there is always another way.

Chapter 1

If You Want To Teach Children To Think

Politics, Hegemony and Holidays In the Dordogne

Ian Gilbert

When you want to teach children to think, you begin by treating them seriously when they are little, giving them responsibilities, talking to them candidly, providing privacy and solitude for them, and making them readers and thinkers of significant thoughts from the beginning. That's if you want to teach them to think.

Bertrand Russell

In 1951, the British philosopher, mathematician and, to be frank, bit of a ladies' man, Bertrand Russell, published an article in the *New York Times* entitled 'The Best Answer to Fanaticism – Liberalism'. For Russell, liberalism isn't about opposing authority but having the freedom to oppose it if you so desire. He doesn't claim that the freedoms to discuss and question will always lead to the best outcomes but that 'absence of discussion will usually lead to the prevalence of the worse opinion'.[1]

Russell's education was as privileged as it was lonely, as is so often the case for our landed gentry. A series of tutors followed by the best that Cambridge University could offer helped develop the man who was undoubtedly one of the greatest thinkers of the 20th century, one who saw critical dissension as much as an exercise required for a good mind as for a functioning democracy.

If this is so, if we do want to teach children to think, and not just to combat fanaticism, to what extent is this actually happening in our classrooms? Are we genuinely fulfilling Russell's dream of treating young people in such a way that their thinking counts? The fact that they should be thinking counting more so? Or can a child perform admirably in a 'successful' school, winning a whole raft of GCSE grades and plaudits without ever having a thought of their own? Could it be argued that the current penchant for the teaching of knowledge in a direct transmission model, regimented by a highly structured system of sanction and control within an equally highly structured school system with its own command, control, measurement and punishment processes in place, is a direct attempt either to get children not to think at all or at least not to think for themselves?

And what about their teachers? Could it be argued that the current predilection for 'education research', the silver bullet to end all silver bullets, is an equally well-designed ploy to prevent educators from thinking for themselves too? Is the push to identify and promulgate 'What works?' a means by which 'What else might work?' can be conveniently overlooked, and the questions 'At what cost?' and 'Works to achieve what?' fail to get a look in?

Which, of course, brings us to the question of hegemony. I don't know about you but this is not a word that cropped up in my teacher training or my classroom teaching career. However, I was uneasy with a French GCSE curriculum that seemed to revolve around a white middle class camping trip to the Dordogne. I was also very concerned that although we didn't set by postcode, if we had it would have made no difference to which children ended up in which set. Looking back, these were all tell-tale signs of hegemony in action, and I was promoting it as blindly as the next person.

Put simply, a cultural hegemony is what you get when the powers that be arrange the world in such a way that it would appear that there is no other way for that world to be so arranged.[2] And then work hard to keep it that way. In education, this is achieved both through *what* is taught and *how* it is taught. In the first instance, a national curriculum is a clearly labelled intellectual land grab that says, 'This is what is important and you must know it'. The inference is, of course, if you know it but it is not in our curriculum, then it is not important.

The fact that in England, at the time of writing, there is a national curriculum, but it is only forced upon those schools which have not followed the yellow brick neo-liberal road to academy status, does not mean that the hegemonic grip is being loosened. Rather, 'they' are holding the dog they are wagging elsewhere – this time through interference in what exam boards put in their schemes of work. Wherever you hold the metaphorical dog – if you are the one deciding, for example, what and whose books are important, what and whose history is important and what constitutes 'British values' – then you control the hegemony and you are very much in the driving seat.[3] No wonder the Secretary of State for Education, Nicky Morgan, rejected a call in 2015 for educators to have at least some say in setting the curriculum, claiming: 'It's my belief that what our children learn in schools must be something that is decided by democratically elected representatives.'[4] We are the hegemon, we get to choose.

In the second instance, with regard to the way children are taught, turning children into uncritical consumers of knowledge ('Because it's in the exam') can well be seen as a process by which we are turning them into uncritical consumers full stop. By definition, citizens do things for the common good and not just for financial or selfish reasons. They make choices, balance views, take responsibility, participate, activate, organise. They think for themselves. It is questionable that a 'sit there and learn what I tell you or else' approach to pedagogy will encourage this, regardless of how well it may prepare young people for passing exams – the only currency of educational success currently in use. Where education and business have become bedfellows, preparing a generation of uncritical consumers seems like a party donation well spent.

Of course, this is not the case in all schools. For the past five years I have spent much of my time as an educator and as a parent in the independent international school sector observing what is effectively the schooling of the children of the developing world's elite. Encouraged by the highly skills-based International Baccalaureate programme, the majority of these schools have independent learning, creativity, leadership and service high on the list of what they promote. Many British nationals I have met working in these schools look with incredulity at the direction English education has taken in the last few years, and I include educators in the very countries that have been held up as great examples to justify this direction, such as Hong Kong, China and Singapore, in that.

So, why is it that some schools are functioning at a very high level by pursuing a progressive, skills-based, child-centred, discovery-driven approach to education whereas state schools in the UK, US and elsewhere are going in the opposite direction? Here is where academic and trenchant observer of the wicked witches of the Western world, Noam Chomsky, has something to say. His view is that education for hoi polloi has always been about 'passivity and obedience', ensuring they know their place, something that is designed to actively deskill them in order to prepare them for life in the factories and offices, to make them, and here he quotes Margaret Thatcher's favourite historical economist Adam Smith, 'as stupid and ignorant as it is possible for a human being to be'. Education for the elite has a very different purpose though: 'It has to allow creativity and independence. Otherwise they won't be able to do their job of making money.'[5]

This is cultural hegemony in action. The system set up by a certain group for a certain order to ensure that the system perpetuates that order. I witnessed this writ large during my time in Chile where a three-tier school system (in order of quality: state schools; subventioned, fee-paying, semi-private schools; fully private schools) both reflected and perpetuated this country's colossal class divides.[6]

In the UK it could be argued that things are a little more subtle, but they are no less powerful for that and just as pervasive and self-perpetuating. And we, the grown-ups in the schools, can be just as much the victims of it as the perpetrators. If you work in a school where the teachers are all middle class and the dinner ladies and site staff aren't, that's the hegemony at work. If you teach in a school where the school leaders are, by majority, white, middle aged, middle class males and the rest of the staff aren't, that's the hegemony. And, as a student, if your school day consists of hearing stories that aren't yours in voices that aren't yours, then that's the hegemony in action too. Which means we must address an important question – what are they learning while you're teaching them?

Fortunately, although we can't escape the hegemony, let alone beat it, we can at least confront it, and it is with the help of one word: *conscientização*.[7] It's a word promoted by the great Brazilian educator Paulo Freire and effectively describes the way in which education, genuine education and not the simple transmission of facts, leads the learner to become conscious of what is really going on. Conscious of cause and effect, of control, of coercion, of oppression, of elitism, of bias, of discrimination, of omission, of selection. Conscious, in a Brazilian nut-shell, of hegemony.

The greatest tool in the arsenal of the teacher who wants to pursue Freire's ideas, and to practice what has become known as 'critical pedagogy',[8] is to simply encourage your students to ask one question – why? With this one question, you can encourage them to dig beneath the surface of the way the world works and begin to learn for themselves *why* it works that way and start to think about *how else* it could be run. There is even research that has found that encouraging 'why' questions leads to the subject expressing more moderate political and religious views which, in our current climate of extreme fear of extremism, would not be a bad thing.[9]

A few months ago I asked the question via Twitter whether teachers felt teaching was a political act. The consensus seemed to be that it was if you wanted it to be. Such a response shows a lack of understanding of what teaching really is, I fear. While the teaching of 'party politics' has little or no place in schools, this is not to be confused with the idea of 'politics' itself, with all that it stands for when it comes to government, law, order, control, persuasion, deception, spin, participation, citizenship, ideals, ethics and values. If you look at politics through this lens then everything a school does – and everything done by every adult in that school – is a political act. All I suggest is that we start to practise such politics with our eyes open.

7

Russell ends his piece for the *New York Times* with what he calls a 'new decalogue' for the liberal teacher. Over 50 years old, it is a set of commandments teachers today would do well to live by. After all, there is a great deal at stake.

1. Do not feel absolutely certain of anything.

2. Do not think it worth while to proceed by concealing evidence, for the evidence is sure to come to light.

3. Never try to discourage thinking for you are sure to succeed.

4. When you meet with opposition, even if it should be from your husband or your children, endeavour to overcome it by argument and not by authority, for a victory dependent upon authority is unreal and illusory.

5. Have no respect for the authority of others, for there are always contrary authorities to be found.

6. Do not use power to suppress opinions you think pernicious, for if you do the opinions will suppress you.

7. Do not fear to be eccentric in opinion, for every opinion now accepted was once eccentric.

8. Find more pleasure in intelligent dissent than in passive agreement, for, if you value intelligence as you should, the former implies a deeper agreement than the latter.

9. Be scrupulously truthful, even if the truth is inconvenient, for it is more inconvenient when you try to conceal it.

10. Do not feel envious of the happiness of those who live in a fool's paradise, for only a fool will think that it is happiness.

If that's the way we approached our professional endeavours, imagine the effect it would have on children when it comes to developing their own thinking. That is, of course, if we want to teach children to think.

Recommended book:

Eduardo Galeano, *Children of the Days: A Calendar of Human History* (London: Allen Lane, 2013)

Notes

1   B. Russell, The Best Answer to Fanaticism – Liberalism, *New York Times* (16 December 1951).

2   Cultural hegemony is an idea most associated with the Italian communist writer Antonio Gramsci. In his *Prison Notebooks* he describes it as, 'The "spontaneous" consent given by the great masses of the population to the general direction imposed on social life by the dominant fundamental group.' However, perhaps the best description of how it works comes from the American author Jacob M. Appel when he writes, 'The most dangerous ideas are not those that challenge the status quo. The most dangerous ideas are those so embedded in the status quo, so wrapped in a cloud of inevitability, that we forget they are ideas at all.' J. M. Appel, *Phoning Home: Essays* (Columbia, SC: University of South Carolina Press, 2014).

3   White history happens all year round; black history gets a month; Arabic history gets nothing.

4   N. Morgan, Everyone Has An Opinion On Education, speech to the ASCL national conference, London, 21 March 2015. Available at: https://www.gov.uk/government/speeches/everyone-has-an-opinion-on-education. The word 'belief' is interesting here. She is not stating a fact, just a useful opinion. What is also interesting from a cultural hegemony perspective is that, of the eight ministers in the Department for Education at the time of her statement, seven were privately educated.

5   N. Chomsky, *Class Warfare: Interviews with David Barsamian* (London: Pluto Press, 1995), pp. 27–31. Quoted at: http://schoolingtheworld.org/resources/essays/education-is-ignorance/.

6 'With a Gini coefficient of 0.51, Chile has the highest level of income inequality after government taxes and transfers among OECD countries.' OECD, Government at a Glance 2013. Country Fact Sheet: Chile. Available at: http://www.oecd.org/gov/GAAG2013_CFS_CHL.pdf.

7 It's a Portuguese one, and one without a direct translation into English, but it does the trick.

8 Comprehensively described by Ira Shor, an American professor and collaborator with Freire, as: 'Habits of thought, reading, writing, and speaking which go beneath surface meaning, first impressions, dominant myths, official pronouncements, traditional clichés, received wisdom, and mere opinions, to understand the deep meaning, root causes, social context, ideology, and personal consequences of any action, event, object, process, organization, experience, text, subject matter, policy, mass media, or discourse.' I. Shor, *Empowering Education: Critical Teaching for Social Change* (Chicago, IL: University of Chicago Press, 1992), p. 129.

9 Science Daily, Answer Three 'Why' Questions: Abstract Thinking Can Make You More Politically Moderate (2 November 2012). Available at: http://www.sciencedaily.com/releases/2012/11/121102151948.htm.

Chapter 2

When Kids REVOLT

Creating the Right Conditions For Powerful Learning

Mark Creasy

Revolt is in the air. Dr Debra Kidd, in her book *Teaching: Notes From the Front Line*, argues, 'We are, at the time I write this, in need of a revolution in education,'[1] and I tend to agree. Teachers need to take back control of the reins before the educational horse finally and irrevocably bolts. One way we can do this is by insisting that there is more to our lessons than simply drilling children full of facts. Much more.

To help reclaim our classrooms, I have put together a process that works very well when it comes to creating quality learning experiences that benefit all learners. While I designed it for my own current area (Key Stage 2), you'll see how applicable it is elsewhere too. It's a process I call REVOLT (see what I did there?) – an acronym that stands for Reassurance, Engagement, Voice, Opportunities, Learning and Time.

The REVOLT approach is simply a guide to help us develop the most effective learning environment for every child. How? By creating carefully structured and crafted projects, not those open-ended tasks with woolly objectives where children 'work together' (i.e. one child does all of the work and others claim the credit for it at the last minute!).

REVOLT projects are different, especially when combining topics, then developing skills and content through them. And they are even better still when they are related to the world around the children, not simply esoteric subject areas. What's more, REVOLT can provide a template for every child in every class, regardless of the individual's academic ability.

So, let's start REVOLTing …

Reassurance

As a starting point, children need reassurance about their skills and abilities. In a high pressured, uncertain world, children need to know they have skills and understand what they are. On top of that they need to be comfortable with having their skills challenged but also reassured that if it doesn't work out, it's not that they are failures, it's just that they used the wrong strategies and need to come at it in a different way next time. As many people have said, influenced by the early research of Carol Dweck, 'You are not your exam results.' These are some of the most important words of reassurance a child can hear, especially if that child is a high achieving student and even more so, according to Dweck, if that child is a girl.

In the best classrooms, REVOLT projects are used to celebrate the children's abilities, but their areas for development are also identified and challenged. The reassurance and support of the teacher, their peers and other adults ensures the secure environment needed for children to progress and develop that all important 'growth mindset'.

Engagement

Let's get one thing straight. The phrase 'You'll need this for the test' does little to develop genuine engagement with, and for, learning. It might get children sitting quietly and getting on with their work but then so does colouring in. REVOLT projects, if cultivated with the children, will naturally draw them in in a deep and lasting way. I love it when children say to me, 'You conned us. I thought this was an easy option, but I've done more work than normal!'

So, how do you go about creating lasting engagement in learning? Well, you start with the end. What is the desired outcome? How will the children be different at the end of the process? Too often great ideas falter by failing to do this. The recent push on computer coding is a case in point, with the 'Let's create an app' idea invariably coming before reflecting on what the children need to/could/should be doing. An app may well provide 'evidence' of their learning, something for the children to work towards and tick the 'We've done technology' box, but why not get the children to create an app as part of their learning, linked to decisions and choices they have made? That way true engagement lies.

Voice

To help with genuine engagement, we need to help learners acquire the language and skills to participate authentically. We need to ensure they have – and use – their voice to let them shape their learning journey. How do they see the link between the curriculum and their lives? Where would they like to take the subject? This voice is something that can be used within the classroom but it should also appear beyond the classroom too. For example, what does your school council really discuss? Do they have autonomy, or do they just bat around ideas that are put to them as a means of box ticking? Is it more 'We appear to give responsibilities' than 'We genuinely value the children's input'?

Opportunities

What opportunities do your children have to see learning as so much more than doing things to pass tests? Where is their variety? What do you allow the children to seek actively and for themselves? One class I taught asked if they could run a newspaper office with all the children taking on various responsibilities. The scheme of work had simply suggested that they should be creating headlines and writing stories, but how much more creative and engaging is this opportunity! When we covered 'ancient civilisations', this time my class asked to create a museum, again with responsibilities for everyone. From the first project the children had learned to ensure a fair distribution of roles for everyone in the second project, something that helped to build confidence in those who didn't naturally see themselves as leaders.

Learning

To help our children REVOLT as we reclaim the classrooms, we need to ensure that their learning is real, relevant and purposeful. It's not only about *what* is learned but also *why* they are learning it (bearing in mind that we have outlawed 'It's for the SATs' in our educational revolution). My maths class recently created self-help guides for each other, using the principle of 'If you can teach someone else, you really understand it'. This included interviewing each other to establish what support they would find most helpful. This meant that one boy who had planned to create step-by-step guides for multiplying two decimals on Prezi was told, 'But I don't like learning that way.' Instead, he successfully applied the Adobe Voice app to meet his partner's preference for verbal instructions (and, before you start frothing at the mouth, this has nothing to do with learning styles – it was just her preference!).

Time

Time is possibly the most precious commodity in schools. My experience is that if you clear away the clutter then you realise you have more of it than you actually thought. I know many colleagues feel that the idea of an uncluttered curriculum is too good to be true; after all, there is so much to fit into the school week. If that's how you feel, then it's certainly time to REVOLT. Extended project time, rather than cramming composite lessons every 45, 50 or 60 minutes, actually serves to clear the clutter.

A great example would be a project I did with my Year 5s, when I asked what we could do to show we understood data, mean, mode, median and graphs through the medium of every teacher's motivational secret weapon – chocolate! For most primary trained teachers that's simple enough by way of a challenge. You'd have to work very hard to make a pig's ear of a project that involved chocolate. However, it was the extent to which the children went beyond the original remit that showed the value of projects combined with trusting the children to take the lead far more than they would do so traditionally. Intended to last three lessons, the project spanned almost two weeks as they built on the original numeracy remit to take in other concepts such as shapes, pie charts, cumulative frequency, volume and surface areas, nets and even money as they worked out profit and loss.

On top of that, they also practically swept the board when it came to including other curriculum areas such as:

* English – branding names, advertising and creating recipes.

* History – chronology, the Aztecs and Spanish and the uses of chocolate.

* Geography – where chocolate comes from.

* Science – the chocolate making process, diet and health.

* Art/tech – designing and making boxes.

* ICT – research, design, presentation.

* MFL – labelling in foreign countries.

* PSHE – the ethical and moral dimension to chocolate. For example, a 13-year-old on a plantation earns 65 pence a day – the value of one bar of chocolate. We also debated whether chocolate should be banned given the UK obesity crisis for children.

There was never any need to tell the children to get on, and they even conducted their own 'unhomework' across the project too, taking it out of the classroom and into the wider world where learning really comes to life. They gained so much by working in this way. We have added a 'genius hour' to the process now, where children can select their topic, related to the subject (something that has been especially successful in maths), and develop their skills and understanding. Areas chosen have included sailing, dogs, high performance cars, places around the world, football and more dogs. It has developed my knowledge of these areas too.

None of this was planned, foreseen or even officially part of the curriculum, nor should it be. Much is being written currently about complexity in learning and how a classroom is – or should be – an 'emergent system'. Working in this way allows children – their characters, their learning, their strengths and their skills – to emerge in a wondrous way.

But don't take my word for it, give it a go. You'll be amazed at what happens when you let the children REVOLT.

Recommended book:

Peter C. Brown, Henry L. Roediger III and Mark A. McDaniel, *Make It Stick: The Science of Successful Learning* (Cambridge, MA: Harvard University Press, 2014)

Notes

1   D. Kidd, *Teaching: Notes from the Front Line* (Carmarthen: Independent Thinking Press, 2014).

Chapter 3

School Libraries and Librarians

Why They Are More Necessary Now Than Ever

Sarah Pavey

'So, what do you do?'

To admit, at a social gathering, that you work as a librarian is to conjure up a vision in the enquirer's mind of a person with a bun and specs who loves reading and who, in a mistaken belief that this is a fancy dress event, has decided to attend dressed as a 'normal' person. Mention that you work in a school, and throw into the mix that your degree is in science rather than the arts, and a clear circle of avoidance arises. Warily those around you back off in case you decide to use your shushing death ray on the conversation and their brief, nervous eye contact with you conveys a palpable sense of pity for a nostalgic character bypassed by the modern world.

Which is interesting because, in the Information Age, librarians are some of the most important people on the planet.

A lot has happened in the world of information over the past century, with the last 10 years seeing an even greater change in the way we produce and access information and the way we communicate with each other to share this new knowledge. It should be a topic ripe for discussion and debate with librarians at the centre. But this image we have is not a good one. If it pervades the whole school community it can result in lost opportunities that affect everyone.

School libraries and librarians (unlike prison libraries) in England are not statutory,[1] they do not have to be inspected by Ofsted and are only mentioned five times in the whole national curriculum (and only then under the 'English' heading). In worst case scenarios the school library is closed and the professional librarian is made redundant or replaced by an unqualified volunteer, something that is more likely to happen in the most socially deprived areas.[2] Maybe this is simply due to ignorance about what a good librarian, with their modern approach to information provision, can create and offer to the school. Maybe the people making the decisions don't go to the right parties.

So what if … a modern librarian – let's call them an information professional – stepped into your school and waved a magic wand to transform the world of information surrounding your students and staff? What if that transformation extended to the furthest reaches of your community? What could they really achieve?

Here are just four areas for consideration.

Space

If you still think that a library is just a physical space within the school then you are mistaken. Much information is accessed online, stored in the cloud and tapped into on a multitude of mobile devices complementing many print sources. In addition, knowledge is likely to be gained through conversation, discussion and collaboration rather than a single teacher spouting forth and notes hurriedly scribbled down without further thought. The library professional has time to create a virtual world, drawing in sources from the public library, online databases and app stores, merging the boundaries with the more familiar codex. They blow the dust from the shelves and get resources used, whether that's fiction fantasy or hard core factual data and, from there, they create space for debate and critical thinking, rather like the Project UnLibrary concept.[3] So the modern library space might be a learning commons area or it might not exist as a separate physical entity at all. All of which means that lack of space can no longer be used as an excuse for not having a library.

Resources

Traditionally resources are costly and perceived as a real financial drain if they remain unused. Indeed, it could be argued that a good set of revision guides and a raft of sample past papers are all that is really needed in an academically successful school (but let's not give 'them' ideas!). But will that arouse curiosity and interest in our students? How will they stand out from the crowd if all the knowledge they obtain is standardised, pre-packaged and delivered in bite-size chunks? How will they learn to use their imaginations and become creative and innovative thinkers in the future – the skills that universities and workplace managers say they need?[4] Carefully chosen library resources fire the intellect and create possibilities and opportunities for everyone. Reading is known to enhance vocabulary,[5] and, let's face it, without word skills, searching the Internet for answers can be very superficial. We need a strong command of language for effective communication. A library professional can select texts, in whatever format, that inspire yet support teaching and learning *and* reading for pleasure. They can ensure that resources are chosen that will be used. Who else in school has the time, the awareness and the skill to undertake such a task effectively?

Finding and using information

With over 700 websites and 72 hours of video uploaded to the Internet *every minute*,[6] maybe you do not need a librarian to find basic information. It's all around us and at our fingertips. But how do you know that what you have found is accurate, factual and to be trusted? We base the progress of our whole existence on the trustworthiness of our ancestors' research, standing on the shoulders of giants. What if our new-found freedom of expression, combined with our ceaseless uploading of unverified data, now makes that academic integrity vulnerable? We readily use Google as our search engine of choice, even bestowing the rare accolade of making a trade name a verb, yet how many of us really acknowledge that it is actually an incredibly clever advertising machine pushing products at us?[7] We choose instead to believe implicitly in the results it shows, rarely criticising or questioning the content. Who teaches the students in your school to examine the information they find, or to use a more sophisticated form of searching to eliminate dubious claims? An information professional can help guide everyone in the school community through this ever expanding information maze to help them reach their goals. It isn't cheating. It's what we do in life, asking for help when we need it from an expert. A librarian is rather like an informational AA man – they can help you and, if they can't, they'll know a man who can. Or a woman. Or a book. Or a website. Or a database. Or a blog. Or an app …

Inspiration and promotion

Teachers are busy people and students are hidebound by relentless testing and learning a specified range of siloed subjects. For librarians, their knowledge area is information and how this can be disseminated to the community. Information professionals have the time to explore and find out about exciting apps, new websites, insightful blogs, useful RSS feeds and, yes, even great books. Furthermore, working within a school setting enables them to understand how what they find applies to the curriculum, schemes of work, the exam syllabus and the school's longer term plans and aims. They can inform everyone using modern social media, a printed newsletter or a digital or physical display. Even better, they can go into classrooms, attend departmental meetings and deliver INSET so that the whole community keeps up to date and, importantly, knows who their librarian is and what they can offer. Rather than just bringing a class to the library for 'research', collaborative lesson planning with assessment criteria that include students demonstrating research skills can reap huge rewards. For example, simply awarding extra marks for presentations not made using PowerPoint encourages students to be creative. The range of alternatives can be demonstrated in class by the librarian. (Senior leaders running an INSET please take note!) Information professionals have circles of practice that stretch beyond the walls of the school – in public libraries, companies, medicine and law, for example – and so can promote exciting ideas developed in school to the wider community and vice versa. Librarians have the time, expertise and connections for such development in a way that other members of staff may not.

A 'library' can be anywhere in a school these days and take whatever form suits the school environment (and budget) best, but the information professional needs to be chosen with care and their skills fully utilised to drive forward new generations of learners and teachers in this time of transformation. A school librarian is not a luxury that can be regarded as an optional extra any more. In the Information Age they are a necessity. As a profession we are no longer caretakers of books but curators of information. We are there to be consulted for help and advice, and we can save the school community hours of precious time. Remember that the next time I meet you at a party, won't you.

Recommended book:

Sharon Markless (ed.), *The Innovative School Librarian: Thinking Outside the Box* (London: Facet Publishing, 2009)

Notes

1   See S. Markless (ed.), *The Innovative School Librarian: Thinking Outside the Box* (London: Facet Publishing, 2009).
2   See All Party Parliamentary Group, *The Beating Heart of the School: Improving Educational Attainment Through School Libraries and Librarians* (London: CILIP, 2014). Available at: http://www.cilip.org.uk/sites/default/files/documents/BeatingHeartoftheSchool.pdf.
3   See https://unlibrary.wordpress.com/.

4   See R. Anderson, *Making Education Work* (London: Pearson, 2014). Available at: http://uk.pearson. com/content/dam/ped/pei/uk/pearson-uk/Campaigns/making-education-work/making-education-work-online-pdf-report.pdf.

5   See A. Sullivan and M. Brown, *Vocabulary From Adolescence To Middle Age*. CLS Working Paper 2014/7 (London: Centre for Longitudinal Studies, 2014).

6   See S. Gunelius, The Data Explosion In 2014 Minute By Minute – Infographic, *ACI* (12 July 2014). Available at: http://aci.info/2014/07/12/the-data-explosion-in-2014-minute-by-minute-infographic/.

7   See I. Miller, The Future of Google ... and Why It's No Longer a Search Company (15 September 2014). Available at: http://www.slideshare.net/millerian/predicting-the-future-of-google-brightonseo.

Chapter 4

The Learning Line

What Goes Up Will Go Down First

Roy Leighton

I have spent the last 20 years of my life working in schools with young people, their teachers, their school leaders, their parents and their communities. I use the same ideas with children in reception or Year 11 that I use with the executives I coach or the business teams I train. Human beings aren't so complicated, not really.

My task, like many before me, has been to tap into the best that is known about how we operate at our best and combine that with my own experience, research and creativity to make it real for today's audiences, whatever their age or circumstances. I try, wherever possible, to follow Einstein's dictum: 'Make things as simple as possible, but not simpler.'

What I have developed, and is now being used effectively in many schools across the UK and abroad, is what I have called the Butterfly Model, and it is some of the thinking behind this idea that I want to share here. But beware. This is not a 'how to' guide. It is not a set of rules. There is no handbook. It is simply a way of looking at the world with wisdom and then acting accordingly on an ongoing basis. The effects can be truly transformational, like the apocryphal butterfly flapping its wings in a South American jungle and instigating a chain of events that lead to a hurricane off the coast of Miami. The smallest of changes can make the biggest of differences in ways you can never predict.

But before we start, let's go back to the beginning. Two primary sources of inspiration have shaped my thinking and practice over the past 30 years and I commend them to any teacher wanting to better understand what they do and how to do it better. Japanese educationalist Tsunesaburō Makiguchi (1871–1944) was an innovative and radical educator whose ideas and practices challenged the very formal Japanese education system at the turn of the 20th century. He believed strongly that learning should be linked to real life and shaped by teachers, not bureaucrats and theorists:

> The task of formulating and clarifying purpose in education cannot be left up to the arbitrary judgment of theoreticians. Rather, the formulation of purpose in education must emerge out of the realities of daily life. It must take into account the entire scope of human life, but at the same time it must consider the specific needs of family, society and nation. The purpose of education, when approached within this kind of comprehensive framework, leads inevitably to happiness as a central framework in human learning.[1]

This desire to dismantle the damaging mechanistic model that had been created by the same minds that had built the factories, prisons and workhouses was a growing global phenomenon. Educators around the world, including Maria Montessori, Rudolf Steiner and John Dewey, declared that the factory model of learning was not only ineffective but was, in many cases, having a negative impact on the learning process and well-being of children. Indeed, this message is still being put forward, with even greater force, by an ever growing army of modern day educators including individuals like Ken Robinson and collaborative educational movements like the one instigated by Ian Gilbert and the team at Independent Thinking. There is far more to education than the setting of exams. There is far more to children than the sitting of exams. It is a contentious point as anyone on Twitter today will tell you!

Makiguchi argued that the purpose of education is to develop the happiness of children by providing an adaptable framework that allows for personalisation and collaboration in the learning process that is directly linked to the community – a community that encompasses each child's family, school, town, country and, ultimately, stretches to the world as a whole.

The second inspiration for me was the work of the American psychologist Dr Clare W. Graves (1914–1986).[2] Gravesian theory identifies a number of stages of maturity at increasing levels of complexity. These 'emergent cyclical levels of existence' are relevant whether we are describing an individual, an organisation, a family or a culture:

> The psychology of the adult human being is an unfolding, ever-emergent process marked by subordination of older behavior systems to newer, higher order systems. The mature person tends to change his psychology continuously as the conditions of his existence change. Each successive stage or level of existence is a state through which people may pass on the way to other states of equilibrium.[3]

I have written elsewhere on the various stages Graves describes to support and develop family dynamics as well as personal and organisational change,[4] but it is worth reflecting here on the six 'conditions of change' necessary in order for maturation to take place. Without them, like a half-decent INSET day, any changes will be limited, short-lived or both. The six conditions are:

1. There must be the *potential* for change.

2. There needs to be a genuine *openness* to find solutions to solve current and previous problems.

3. We need to accept and embrace the fact that *dissonance* within the individual and organisation is always going to be an outcome of any change process.

4. There must be a willingness and ability to honestly identify and deal with the *barriers* (individually, collectively and environmentally) to change.

5. We must be open to emerging *insights* into what hasn't worked and/or what the possible alternatives could be.

6.   There must be *consolidation* and support throughout this dynamic process.

One tool I have developed that is proving to be very useful as teachers take these ideas into their classrooms is the Learning Line. It's simple, but not too simple. For example, one 4-year-old I worked with in Leeds, having been shown the Learning Line as a process to show their own learning journey, independently drew the Learning Line and then went to find the teacher to discuss how they could make progress. It's not rocket science.

The Learning Line then develops to higher levels of complexity as the children progress through levels of maturity and challenge. From a simple line with smiley faces for early years, the Learning Line becomes the Hero's Journey and moves into a whole new level of imagination, possibility and challenge.[5]

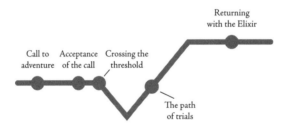

The Hero's Journey.

If you believe government and Ofsted rhetoric on how children learn you would think that it is a continuous straight line that starts at stupid (i.e. empty of the requisite facts and skills) and ends at educated (replete with facts and some skills). If an inspector doesn't witness learner progress in the snapshot of the lesson they see, then it was not a good lesson according to this thinking. Yet going backwards *is* progress when viewed through the lens of the Learning Line. And once children grasp that falling down is an essential part of moving on, it can transform their attitude to learning, their self-motivation, their resilience and their achievements in the classroom and beyond.

The Learning Line works for organisations, it works for classes and it works for individuals to plot where they are both in an academic subject but also in learning a new skill or dealing with situations outside of school. I have worked with whole staff groups where we have plotted the position of the school in its growth. I have worked with groups of 5-year-olds where we have worked out where the class is on its journey. I have worked with individual children who have marked where they are on their (laminated) Learning Lines, how they got there, where they want to go and what it will take to get there.

Learning is a complex, emergent system where small changes can change everything. By understanding and *applying* some core principles about what makes us human and how we grow, we don't so much as make learning happen as let it happen. And I highlight the term 'applying' with good reason. Unless the ideas shared here are put into practice, we may be no more than those very people that Makiguchi warned would block the development of a truly values-based, human and humane system of education. The theoreticians, academics, institutions and self-seeking career builders who have lost their purpose and seek merely to give the impression of beauty, goodness, gain and truth when in reality they are, by doing nothing, blocking the emergence of the system that can create, in a very practical way, an educational experience that does in reality that which they only talk about.

So, go for it and remember, knowledge is not an indication of ability. In the words of the Buddha, 'If you know, but do not do, you do not know.'

Recommended book:

Charles Handy, *The Second Curve: Thoughts on Reinventing Society* (London: Random House Business, 2015)

Notes

1 T. Makiguchi, *The System of Value-Creating Pedagogy* (Soka kyoikugaku taikei), 4 vols (1930).

2 For more information visit: http://www.clarewgraves.com/.

3 C. C. Cowan and N. Todorovic (eds), *The Never Ending Quest: Dr Clare W. Graves Explores Human Nature* (Santa Barbara, CA: ECLET Publishing, 2005), p. 29.

4 See S. Bowkett, T. Lee, T. Harding and R. Leighton, *Happy Families: Insights Into the Art of Parenting* (London: Network Continuum Education, 2008); R. Leighton, E. Kilbey and K. Bill, *101 Days To Make a Change: Daily Strategies To Move From Knowing To Being* (Carmarthen: Crown House Publishing, 2011).

5 The Hero's Journey is the theory put forward by writer and mythologist Joseph Campbell that stories throughout time have followed a basic 17-point pattern that starts with 'The Call to Adventure' and ends with 'Freedom to Live'. It is a powerful device when used in schools to help children become their own heroes. See J. Campbell, *The Hero With a Thousand Faces* (Princeton, NJ: Princeton University Press, 1949).

Chapter 5

Live Your Life

And 19 Other Things I Wish I'd Known When I Started Teaching

Rachel Jones

1. Children aren't data. Even though data is easier to manage than children, don't be tempted to favour it over nurturing meaningful relationships in school.

2. You will never know the struggles and difficulties that children are facing in a classroom. Don't expect every child to come with a label. And don't treat children as if the labels they come with are all they are. Every single child in your classroom will do something amazing over the year. It is your job to know them well enough to be able to spot and then celebrate the victories and triumphs – no matter how big or small. Poverty and disinterest do more to grind down children than you can imagine. We are not in a position to solve poverty because we are teachers. But, because we are teachers, we need to do all we can to help children living in it.

3. Learning cannot be quantified. Unless you first qualify what learning is.[1]

4. Be your own teacher. Learn to be yourself. Remain true to the people who inspired you to go into teaching. If you find yourself putting on a show for a lesson observation, remind yourself that your children deserve more than a fraud and you are more than a fraudster. I once read that a teacher is 'no better than their last observation grade'.

What an indictment of a system that categorises people as a number and doesn't see either their true worth or their potential.

5. Schools are full of rules but it is easier to ask for forgiveness than seek permission. You won't even know what some of the rules are until you break them yourself. Don't be frightened to do things differently and welcome that the children you teach might also do the same.

6. The stakes are high in education, not just in terms of attainment but also in terms of your credibility. Children deserve meticulous planning as well as a teacher who is brave enough to throw the lesson plan away. I was teaching sixth formers on the day of the London bombings in 2005. Continuing with a mock exam on that day would have been disrespectful and insensitive.

7. Don't hold grudges against subjects you didn't like when you were at school.

8. If you have a reward system in school that only praises conformity, you are missing the opportunity to celebrate the many hundreds of things that make us unique. Staff and learners need to be rewarded for more than obedience.

9. Whole school responsibility is a funny thing. You are in a position to make meaningful and, maybe, much needed change, but it isn't easy. You will be blamed for things that are out of your control, and be asked to enact change with little regard for time or financial constraints. Remember to share the burden. Real responsibility needs to be shared, not just shouldered.

10. Really brilliant teaching looks different for every teacher. It looks different for every class. It even looks different depending on what time of day it is. Be sensitive. Adapt. There is no 'what works' rulebook.

11. The most important thing that you can do for your students is care. A very close second is to ignite the spark that makes them curious about the world – and that they, in turn, care enough to do good in it.

12. Be polite to everyone in school. They are all trying to do their job, just like you are.

13. Choose what battles you fight. Pick what really matters. Be prepared to play the long game when it comes to the achievement of your students. In my experience, quick fixes don't fix anything really important.

14. Using technology in your lessons can be magical and inspiring. So can a pen and paper. Know when to use which and when to use none of them.

15. It is not our job as teachers to make learning easy. Handing out worksheets isn't teaching. Teaching is about being more than just the grown-up who tells kids what to do. It is about more than just getting kids to behave. And it is definitely about more than just getting kids to know things that they can regurgitate for an exam or essay. That might be what you are paid for, but where is the magic in that?

16. Secondary teachers have a lot to learn from their colleagues in the primary sector. Don't discount their work. Ever. If you are wondering why your Year 7s seem to become demotivated soon after arriving at your secondary school, go and spend a day at the feeder primary school. You'll soon see why.

17. Schools can be exam factories. To combat this, take pleasure in the simple things that can make everyone's day better. Is it sunny? Go outside and learn. Is it Friday? You really need to get a Cake Friday rota going …

18. On bad days remember it will get better. If you have a lot of bad days then seek support and help. There is nothing wrong with admitting you are struggling; after all, this is about you acting in the best interests of your students.

19. Don't talk *at* kids. Talk *to* them. Don't do things *to* kids. Do things *with* them. Don't do things *for* kids that they can do for *themselves*.

20. Your job is not your life. It is part of your life. Work hard. Enjoy it. But don't let it consume your life outside of school. Live your life too. This is especially true if you are in the leadership team. It sets a good example.

Recommended book:

Avital Ronell, *The Telephone Book: Technology – Schizophrenia – Electric Speech* (Lincoln, NE: University of Nebraska Press, 1989)

Notes
1   Thanks to MW for clarification.

Chapter 6
How To Paint a Better School
Why School Improvement Is Not a Numbers Game

Dave Harris

Have you ever seen a 'paint by numbers' version of Constable's *The Hay Wain*? I have. To be fair, you can see what it's supposed to be. It even has most of the same elements of the original. Yet even in the hands of a skilled practitioner it will never be more than a pale shadow of the genuine work of art. Now, of course, few people will be surprised by this revelation. Sticking to the lines on a predetermined path using a limited set of colours does not a masterpiece make.

Copying something great gives someone with no artistic flair a sense of achievement, I grant you. Otherwise painting by numbers would never have been so popular. But once the paint is dry and the smell of thinners has faded, what you are left with is a copy of a copy of a copy – and a numbing sense that maybe there is more to creating great art than this.

If the copying of copies by those with little skill or imagination isn't really good enough for great art, then why does it increasingly seem to be the methodology for education? It appears to me that there is a growing view in education (and yes, academy chains, I'm looking at you especially) that a painting by numbers approach to creating successful schools is the way forward. Replace the paints with a standard uniform policy, a ready-made discipline structure and teacher's rulebook, and the job's done.

But once the ink has dried on the glossy new brochure, what you are left with is a copy of a copy – and a numbing sense that there must be more to creating great schools than this.

As a former head in a small academy chain (and that's a story in itself but I'll save it for my memoir!), I have heard some academy leaders talk about their plans for expansion and world domination with a self-interest and self-satisfaction that I found quite sickening. (Imagining Mr Burns from *The Simpsons* in charge of a group of schools will help you get the picture.) Their logic is that because their school has experienced some degree of exam success then they must be doing things the 'right way', a way that can be copied ad infinitum to turn every school they touch into a masterpiece.

Such an approach to school improvement has all the finesse, subtlety and artistic merit of painting *The Hay Wain* by numbers. They take the outline from their 'success' as the picture needed for each and every school they are taking over. This outline is then presented as a non-negotiable grid for their design – you either help paint the picture this way or you'll have your paintbrush unceremoniously snapped in half at staff briefing. Sticking inside the lines is crucial for this plan to work, but I suggest that hardly any aspect of real life works best when you stick within the lines. And this is all the more the case when you are working with children. Draw a line and most children – not to mention their talented teachers – will want to cross it. In fact, my experience has shown me that great teaching almost certainly involves removing the lines altogether as teachers develop their own way, and great leadership is the process by which you support and encourage this.

Most of the great teachers and school leaders I have met – and there are many, despite the difficulties of colouring outside the lines in the current climate of control, coercion and fear – didn't come into the job to peddle some corporate message. They were drawn to the profession to make a difference, to help young people blossom into talented and happy adults. This might sound idealistic stuff, but how else would we be able to put up with all the rubbish we are expected to face if we couldn't see past that to a greater goal?

For me, I always wanted to create a masterpiece, something that would make people stand back and think, something of lasting beauty and power, something that would make a difference. I didn't always succeed but I'm glad I tried. And I'm glad I tried without following someone else's lines. My saddest moments were working with people who didn't share my desire to make a permanent change that was unique to a school and its community. Too many narrow-minded and soulless individuals seem to be crowding into the areas around educational leadership and school ownership, talking of quick wins and claiming instant solutions.

I still believe that any school, indeed any community, is capable of producing its own unique masterpiece with the power to change the way people think, especially if it is given the time to develop it. As I have written elsewhere, it's a marathon, not a sprint.

So, to extend the painting analogy, here are some quick art lessons that you can use to paint yourself a masterpiece the whole community can be proud of:

1. Before you start work on the canvas imagine what it could be like. Sketch some possibilities without rushing into making that all important first stroke. Think about the composition that would best suit the intended location. Remember that each location demands a different masterpiece – even the *Mona Lisa* wouldn't look right on every wall.

2. Choose the best quality materials you can afford. Maximise your chances for producing something impressive and long lasting. Ensure quality staff are motivated and keen to make their mark, and that they are given the resources, support and space to do so.

3. Then, and only then, start building your masterpiece with a colour-wash of your ethos and beliefs to give a true basis for your work and a few outline shapes to form the structure. But beware the temptation to get out the big brush and complete the picture too quickly. And be cautious of thinking you can finish the picture by yourself too. It

is vital to gain the opinions of others at this point. Many a great work is ruined by too much ego and too little consultation and empathy.

4. Now for the long haul. Begin developing the colour and texture of each part of your painting. Remember, if you use too many bold and dark colours they are difficult to remove or paint over in the future. A master knows that light colours may not immediately have the desired effect but, once the painting progresses, their early application comes to add subtlety to the work.

5. Don't forget to take a step back to admire your work as often as possible and check that it is developing as you originally planned. Revisit your original hopes and desires and check that you haven't lost your way. Make sure that you frequently share your progress with those for whom it was intended. It is no good having a masterpiece that doesn't meet the requirements of the very people you painted it for.

Of course, all of this takes time, and no one expects it to happen overnight. Well, when I say no one, I clearly mean anyone who understands the complexity and importance of the job we do. There are some who still believe that the best solution is the printed board and a set of eight little tubs of paint. They see learning like a production line with inputs, outputs and standardised processes. And children, well, they're the widgets.

It breaks my heart that this isn't a joke. I have met these people. The world is a simple place for them and they believe they have the 'successful school picture' all drawn out, numbered off and ready for lesser mortals to simply fill in the colours. But rather than following the numbers we need to stand up and be counted. This approach is simply not good enough for schooling. We demand that all our young people – and their teachers – have the opportunity to create of their school and their lives their own work of art.

Recommended book:

Margaret Wheatley, *Leadership and the New Science: Discovering Order In a Chaotic World* (San Francisco, CA: Berrett-Koehler, 2001)

Chapter 7

Educational Research

The Eternal Search

Dr Phil Wood

In recent years there has been an explosion of interest in the use of research in schools. This has particularly been the case where effect sizes are concerned, the work of John Hattie being the most well-known. The reliance on effect sizes is part of a wider 'what works' approach to research which appears to be gaining popularity in schools. A 'what works' approach rests on the assumption that certain research methodologies can be used to unearth optimal ways of teaching, or the best way of approaching a particular pedagogic activity.

In the present educational environment this has a ready appeal. In a system that expects constant improvement and progress, coupled with a data driven approach to professional development, the idea of being able to identify pedagogic activities that are 'proven' to make a difference is attractive. However, this perspective on research makes two important assumptions: firstly, that there is an identifiably 'best' way of teaching and, secondly, that teaching is a reductive pursuit with little, or no, ethical or professional input, reducing the teacher to a technician.

In a 'what works' agenda, where are judgement and context located?

Whilst a 'what works' approach to research might be perceived as positive because it can take up little or no teacher time to embed in school planning, it also means that research outcomes might become blindly accepted, with little understanding of the methods used or critical engagement to assess the arguments made. There is the danger that the results of research become 'imported' into practice with little reflection or critique. This lays teachers open to the possibility of embedding poor research as they have little foundation on which to assess the validity and utility of research findings.

Hopefully, the aim of engaging with research is to extend and improve practice through critical engagement and understanding, thereby fostering positive reflection and judgement in how research findings are enfolded into action. If this genuinely is the focus of engagement with research, there is a need to establish and generate research literacy within schools. Yet research literacy is not a simple or universally defined term.

I would argue that it has three elements. Firstly, a knowledge and understanding of research methods and data analysis/interpretation. Secondly, a conceptual dimension which underpins the other aspects of research literacy. This includes an understanding of concepts such as 'methodology' and 'ethics', which are central to designing and carrying out research projects as well as engaging with the research accounts of others. Finally, there is the practice of research. After all, one of the best ways of developing an understanding of research is to carry out research yourself, thereby gaining practical experience of how research fits together and makes sense.

So what might a blueprint for research in schools look like?

Research is multifaceted, particularly so in education as it is an interdisciplinary field. This means that many different approaches to research have developed over time, from large scale studies that are often quantitative in nature to small scale case studies, and from experimental or evaluative studies to exploratory research – for example, action research.

In the recent rush to take an interest in educational research, some of these approaches, particularly small scale and exploratory research, have been criticised as being too anecdotal or the result of 'cargo cults'. However, one of the first moves towards literacy in research is to recognise that these different approaches are attempting to achieve different things, and therefore to understand their contributions they need to be understood on their own terms. Criticising a case study as 'anecdotal' is to miss the point, as it is not attempting to generalise in the same way as a much larger study but to give deep insight into an identified context. Its use is in acting as an explanatory starting point for discussion by others rather than as a blueprint for universal activity.

To make critical use of research findings we need to invest in gaining knowledge, understanding and a conceptualisation of the breadth of educational research traditions. We need to be able to assess the interpretations of data in relation to the methodology of the project. We need to have a good level of knowledge if we are to make such claims with any certainty. But to really understand how research methodologies fit together and how they relate to data analysis and interpretation, as well as the inherent practical complexity of completing a research project, we need to undertake our own research. Only experience can help us understand how to create, conduct and critically engage with research. Therefore, if schools really want to make positive use of research, they need to undertake their own work – work that has meaning and utility *in their own context*.

Research literacy comes from slow, consistent engagement with the research process. It can be argued that schools and teachers have neither the time nor the desire to be involved in research, and this is a wholly reasonable argument. However, within any school, not all teachers need to be active in the same way, and not all need to be involved in conducting primary research. In addition, in many schools there might be a very small pool of research experience. This is why if research is to play a sustainable role in schools it needs to be seen as a collaborative process. It should rest on collaboration between individuals within a school, and through collaboration with other schools and external partners, especially universities, which have a wealth of expertise they can offer in supporting the development of research literacy.

Remember, research can only ever inform and offer insights into possible practices. If you believe research can present a set of perfect tools and immutable practices, a rulebook for pedagogy, you'll be sorely disappointed, because that is not its aim. It is a framework to help question, explore and gain insights into educational problems and issues, to offer ideas and starting points for better practice. It cannot do more than this in the eternal search for the perfect pedagogy!

Recommended book:

Clive Opie, *Doing Educational Research* (London: Sage, 2004)

Chapter 8

Because It's In the Exam

Why We Need To Teach Beyond the Test

Lisa Jane Ashes

I had been asked to redesign our school's Key Stage 3 curriculum and I thought, why not? What's the worst that can happen? Actually, what happened was that it totally transformed my understanding of what school was about. Rather than looking at making a change to a few fairly unimportant secondary school years (or so it seems to many schools), I suddenly came to realise what a disjointed and dysfunctional process schooling children really is.

Seeing things through the children's eyes, I realised that their school life pretty much entails walking from one classroom to another, five times a day, five days a week, learning new things, then leaving the new learning behind as they move to yet another segregated subject in another part of the school. When asked why they are taught each topic, children reply in unison, 'Because it's in the exam'. When asked why they teach each topic, teachers reply in unison, 'Because it's in the exam'. And at the end of 12 years, there it is, the exam, and then, whoosh, the process of educating them is over.

It feels like we have always done it this way. So why change?

Our world has always changed but now it is changing at an exponential rate. I know you've heard that before but stop and think about it. Change really is happening faster, yet our schools were designed for a time when things, although not static, were certainly more fixed and certain. That's why you could have textbooks that lasted for years. My biggest fear is that if we keep delivering such a disjointed, outmoded secondary education, with no visible purpose beyond 'It's in the exam', the disengagement of those most in need of education will only grow.

To be fair, education in England has a history of refusing to adapt. In Renaissance England, things were also changing pretty quickly with new geographical studies, philosophies and physical enquiries being pursued. Yet, Renaissance England's schools refused to budge. The curriculum (only available for the upper classes – the poor knew their place and had little need for reading or writing anyway) remained narrowly focused around religious texts.

When we reached the Industrial Revolution, society opened its eyes to what was going on. England's population boomed as new technologies in agriculture and manufacturing changed the way people worked and lived. Children as young as 2 went to school so that their parents could go out to work. These new 'minding schools' were a reaction to the need for childcare, not a well-thought-out plan for the future. It was a common belief that our poorest citizens should not be taught too much lest they become dissatisfied with their lot in life. 'Monatorial schools' were, like the country, industrialised. The introduction of standard repetitive practices allowed hundreds of children to be taught at once. Great for an overcrowded population that needed basic schooling in the three Rs to suit the needs of an industrialised country. Hardly inspiring for those enduring it.

Perhaps the 'success' of industrialised schools is why today's education remains stuck in that era of uniformity. We are led to believe that one size fits all. The uniform, linear examination of segregated subjects remains. Subject specialists work alone to fill with facts the heads of the many, leading to overloaded minds and disengaged children.

Cognitive load theory (probably taught to you during your professional qualification but you may have been so overloaded with other information that you have forgotten it) suggests that our working memory is limited. There is only so much that we can take in at once before we have to start pushing other stuff out – like the ichthyology professor who would forget the name of a fish each time he learned the name of a new student. But how helpful is it for our pupils to have so much disjointed information loaded into their developing minds? If you can hold vast amounts of information and regurgitate it in just the right way, you are awarded a disembodied grade. How many of our country's children are let down by this old fashioned, unrealistic system? How many children are educated for 12 years and leave with nothing? The history of education in England tells the same story as far back as it can be traced – education failing to adapt, a trend of failure for the poor.

Many children opt out, physically or mentally, often verbalising how utterly pointless school is until the day they are permitted to leave. If you've ever had to convince children who can barely read of the merits of learning Shakespeare, you'll know what I mean. And it is our poorest children who still lag behind the most, as highlighted by the 2013 policy paper, *Education, Justice and Democracy* by Professor Stephen Ball:

> *Despite the relentless and repeated criticisms of state schooling and the ongoing reform of the school system, the relationships between opportunity, achievement and social class have remained stubbornly entrenched and have been reproduced by policy. Inequalities of class and race remain stark and indeed have been increasing since 2008.*[1]

Think about how it was for you when you were at school. In the 1990s, the lessons that I was being taught never felt applicable to the world I was living in. Adults just didn't understand. In a similar way to how curriculums are arranged now, individual subjects were competing for space in my head and I didn't have any idea (or, critically, any inclination) to stop the information from spilling out of my ears. That was me then; imagine pupils now.

For me, as I drudged through school, I would dream of being somebody some day as my way of escaping the monotony of school life. These days, children don't have to dream about being somebody some day when they can be someone else and do that today thanks to social media. Escape, reward and gratification are delivered in a way that their education does not seem able to understand. Why work hard for good exam results when you have thousands of followers on Twitter, Instagram or whatever social media is the next big, cool trend? Young people don't need to wait until the end of their school life for recognition when likes, follows and other forms of recognition can make them feel good today. The instant gratification delivered by the digital world in their hands feels so much better than the boring, hard, unrelated and pointless lessons they have to sit through in school.

We need to rethink education for so many reasons. We are overloading brains, wasting time – ours and theirs, failing to teach for today, let alone tomorrow, and allowing thousands of children to disengage as a result, especially the most vulnerable. The Digital Revolution, like the Industrial Revolution, is in danger of going down in English history as yet another failure to get education right for its time. If we react as we did to the Industrial Revolution, we are in danger of digitalising our classrooms with no greater purpose than a gut response to reflecting an era. Throwing iPads at classrooms may re-engage our pupils for a moment, but if we don't get our heads together they'll soon switch back to Facebook and continue to see education as a waste of time.

We need to shape our children today for what will come their way tomorrow. We need to open their eyes to the purpose – and purposefulness – of education beyond simply examinations. We need to teach them to apply their learning effectively to the complexities of a future world. Manglish was my reaction to one school's disjointed, old fashioned curriculum where I combined literacy and numeracy to be taught across the secondary curriculum. But it needs to get a whole lot bigger than that. Come away from your subject specialism for a moment. Look, as I did, at your curriculum through the eyes of the children and ask, 'What are we educating them for?' If the answer is, 'Because it's in the exam', we need to rethink the whole thing.

Recommended book:

Daniel T. Willingham, *Why Don't Students Like School? A Cognitive Scientist Answers Questions About How the Mind Works and What It Means For the Classroom* (San Francisco, CA: Jossey-Bass, 2010)

Notes

1   S. Ball, *Education, Justice and Democracy: The Struggle Over Ignorance and Opportunity* (London: Centre for Labour and Social Studies, 2013), p. 4.

Chapter 9

The Values Seesaw

Or How To Balance Your Own View of What's Right With the Demands of the System and the Pressures Placed On Us From 'Above'

Dave Whitaker

As the head of a special school, I am often met with the same look by my mainstream colleagues. It's a combination of awe ('I couldn't do your job'), bemusement ('Why would anyone do your job?') and dismissal ('Just don't tell me how to do my job'). But bear with me, there are some things that happen in special schools and pupil referral units (PRUs) that are actually very good. In fact, it could even be said they are excellent. Let's go one step further and coin a term used by our, er, friends at Ofsted and say they are actually outstanding.

Special schools cover a vast spectrum of provision and I will never claim to be a special needs expert. However, when it comes to behaviour I feel that I have a few things to say, a few experiences to share and can offer some insights into one of the most daunting and terrifying aspects of a teacher or school leader's life.

The first thing to understand is that although my school is not your normal school setting, it is still a school. And, as should be the case in all schools, we believe that every child deserves the very best care, attention, support, guidance and, dare I say it, love[1] we can give them as caring professionals. Get this lot right and the education follows. Get this lot right and the behaviour changes. Get this lot right and the children prosper. Provide the appropriate environment with the appropriate people doing appropriate things and the children will progress. And I don't mean 'make progress' in an Ofsted way. I mean genuinely improve. Children with chaotic lives, with high levels of vulnerability and seriously low aspirations and self-esteem can, and will, succeed if we play our part right. They just need to be ready to learn. Yet, if that is the case, why are so many children with challenging behaviour not succeeding in school? Why are more and more children ending up in PRUs, and why are behavioural, emotional and social difficulties (BESD) schools full?

The answers are manifold.

For a start, the pressure from Ofsted makes some teachers and school leaders do what they might not want to do, or even feel is the morally correct thing to do. But they do it anyway. League tables and exam results exert the same kind of corrupting influence. The lack of genuine contextualised accountability puts disproportionate levels of pressure on some schools in very challenging communities. Behaviour in schools is such a contentious issue that it causes otherwise level headed, highly principled and wonderful school leaders to make decisions that could be deemed out of character, rash, immoral or even foolish. School leaders at all levels who would normally and happily embrace collaboration and inclusion can become selfish, underhand and even sneaky. I've seen it.

Take a look at any school website and you will find a string of promises, mission statements and values. These are there to reassure parents that their school of choice will look after everyone and that every child will succeed. And that includes their child. But is this true? Really?

Imagine a seesaw. On one side sit the values of the school (which often reflect the values of the head teacher or, increasingly so in recent times, those of the academy chain). On the other sit the 'school systems'. Too often, the tremendous pressure exerted by the various elements of the system outweighs the values the school is trying to live by. When this happens the system wins and some of our most vulnerable children suffer. As a school leader, your job is to make sure this does not happen.

If you truly have a values driven approach to leading your classroom, or your school, then surely one of the first things you must do is address this imbalance. The challenge is to make sure that your values outweigh the systems. Always. Without fail. How do you do this? Well, this is the brave bit. If the systems look like they are tipping the balance then you change them. You stand by your values and you adapt your systems.

I know this can prove very difficult when it comes to classroom behaviour. Behaviour is like the burning Eye of Sauron in *The Lord of the Rings*. It seeks out weakness and it punishes it – in teachers, personalities, leaders, systems, buildings, curricula, lesson plans, resources, timetables, lunchtimes, school buses, accreditation and so on. In fact, there is nowhere the Eye cannot see. That is why PRUs and special schools are full. That is why we need to do something about it. That is why we all need to face this challenge full on. That is why we need to understand it, change things and take responsibility. And do so at all levels.

So, where do you start? Well, you have a choice when it comes to behaviour management in your school and it is simple. You either use sanctions, which ultimately lead to a child being kicked out of school when these sanctions fail to work, or you put in the time and the effort, the professionalism and the expertise, to support the child and change their behaviour for the better. After all, it is either your problem to deal with or it's someone else's. And if you genuinely think that the behaviour of your children is someone else's problem then it's time to wake up and smell the roses!

Behaviour is everyone's issue. It impacts on us all. It keeps us awake at night. It forces decent, hard-working people out of our fantastic profession and can even lead to emotional breakdown and depression. Without us all doing our bit then there will be no end to it. We all need to work together, to take collective responsibility and do whatever we can to change things, not just pass them on to someone else.

One way we can do this is by taking an enquiry approach to dealing with challenging behaviour. The main premise here is whatever they do, there is always a reason for it (the same can be said of all human beings – not just children). If you look at behaviour as a symptom you start to move from questions like 'Why won't they behave?' to 'Why aren't they behaving?' That leads you down a very different route. So, try to find out why a child is behaving in a certain way and then do something about it.

For example, think about the child who never has a pen. Every time he comes to school without a pen he gets a detention. He gets a detention every week for not bringing a pen. That child merely factors detention into his weekly routine and accepts it as part of his way of life. But, you know what, he doesn't actually own a pen. He lives in a house where there are no pens, and there are no pens because actually nobody at home can write. His parents won't buy him a pen because they are too drunk to leave the house and they don't actually care anyway.

So, over to you as the professional. Are you looking at the detention data for your school? Are you noticing the number of pupils who seem to continually have detentions? Are you asking yourself if you are really dealing with behaviour or merely plastering over the cracks?

Don't get me wrong. I am all for consequences, and pupils must take responsibility for their actions. Standards must be high and expectations equally so. However, children must also be helped and supported in their behavioural development. If a child has not yet learned to read then we look at why they can't read yet and we teach them. We don't put them in detention or exclude them. So, if a child has not yet learned how to behave, why do we punish them until we run out of suitable punishments then simply pass them on to someone else?

I seem to remember that someone once said 'every child matters'. Were they right? If they looked at your school would that be true? So, please think about behaviour – yours as well as theirs – and think about what you can do to make a difference. Without your passion, commitment and resilience, thousands of pupils will continue to be failed on a daily basis in our schools. Now, you wouldn't want that for your students, would you?

Recommended book:

Louise Bomber and Daniel A. Hughes, *Settling Troubled Pupils to Learn: Why Relationships Matter in School* (Duffield: Worth Publishing, 2013)

Notes

1   You can use the term 'unconditional positive regard' if you prefer. It has the same effect.

Chapter 10

Rules For Mavericks

When Teachers Are Caught Thinking For Themselves

Phil Beadle

'Maverick' is not a title you award yourself. There are, so I've been told, a number of things more humiliating than waking up from an evening on the tiles, wondering what the hell you did last night, to come, eventually, to the confused, half-remembered recollection of listing hopelessly to starboard in some bar or other stridently declaiming that you are an unapologetic maverick; then, recalling, in both revulsion and horror, that, immediately after this, you hiccoughed, burped and collapsed into a spewing pool of your devastated self-esteem. There are a number of things more humiliating than this, few so richly pitiful.

'Maverick' is not a title you award yourself. It will be thrown in your direction if you meet certain conditions, the first of which is that you do not ever seek it. The second is that you will (always, ever) have an entirely ambiguous relationship with the badge.

'Maverick' is not a title you award yourself. A true maverick does not seek (and has only ever rarely sought out of either upset or bloody-mindedness caused by that upset) marginalisation; they have always regarded their ideas as having a fairly unarguable logic, a mainstream appeal and a hooky enough chorus, and will be initially offended by the title. Your first experience (or memory) of the word may be of your pathetic, stuttering reaction to its intended assault; a memory of standing, your sweating back stuck to your shirt, as you retreated, under fire, into some bland institutional wall, having been in receipt of its tepid accusatory slaughter for the first time. 'Maverick' is word as arrow. That is why it exists. That is its purpose. It is designed to wound.

However, after long decades of having been identified by this grotesque lapel badge of a word, you might finally give up seeking the acceptance of the dull and seek, instead, to reconcile yourself to being distanced from acceptable norms. You might wonder how, given that you cannot escape the pointing finger of the word's assault, you might try to be as good an outsider as possible. You might choose, given that the mainstream rejects you, to live the best version of life on the margins you are able to. The question is, if you are to be identified as left field, how do you do this as well as it is possible to do? And, I suppose, that is what this book is for: to help you turn pariah status into something that works for you. If you are unable to conform, then – you may as well face up to it – you are unable to conform. You will have to find ways outside of the path of *mean* average.[1]

First, however, let us look at why you are in receipt of this accusation. What does it mean? Or, rather, what motivates the accusation? In bald answer to the first question, 'maverick' is a word that conformists use to diminish and ostracise those for whom the skill of conformity is too ugly a proposition to be (in any way) a romantic possibility; the term 'maverick' is there to let you know that you are intellectually homeless, that there is no real place for you in institutional life; you cannot be a success on the terms of engagement as they are, and should be ashamed of this, and of yourself.

Your first experience of this word might be to have it spat at you with a mild expletive attached, the intent of which is to mock. As in, 'You're such a bloody maverick.' It is not a compliment, and you should not take it as such. It is a sign that the 'freeness' of your thought (which will be presented as – and may in fact be – an inability) is somehow letting the side down. Your maverick nature will be presented as a flaw; a deficiency; a weakness; a hole in the *you* that you will be made to wish was not there, but is; it is the ineffective comb-over of a liver-spotted bald patch; a rampant disease of the ego; a pity and a waste; it is evidence of something they had always suspected: an inability to do what you are told by your betters, who will usually have expressed their superiority through the agency of a grey business suit (real or metaphorical); it is evidence that your face doesn't fit, your jib is cut unappealingly and how you do things is summarily and emphatically not, 'The way we do things round here.'

And all of these things are true.

Under the rules as they are.

In this particular institution, and probably in all institutions. (You may have to create your own.)

The most minute of glances at institutional life leads us to one sure conclusion: bullies prosper here. Any form of religious devotion is merely mental illness on a global scale (a deviant intelligence gene that propels poor humans to seek some paltry comfort in ritual, though that ritual is palpably insane). You can argue that intelligent design exists, however. While religions might have been constructed for some other purpose than to keep the poor cowed, obedient and accepting of their fate as slaves, clearly, those with access to the keys to the cathedral have intelligently designed a way of using obedience to the hierarchies that organised religion implies to their profit. So it is in institutional life. Those who have risen to the heights of the enviable job title[2] are those who have profited most from saluting the book of acceptable behaviour(s), and are generally, therefore, those who lean most acutely towards adherence to unquestionable dogma.

Let us have a look at your accuser. She is a successful person in her way. She has a nice home that she may struggle to afford and a family she cannot afford either. She is under pressure: her family is reliant on the job, she has risen to the ranks of management because she is good at the job. (She may be redundant at 50, never to work again, to dissipate her remaining years, as regret eats her.) But for now she follows the rules. She plays by the book. She didn't get where she is today by flagrantly disregarding the tradition of the form,[3] or thinking that she could forge a completely new path through it. She is under pressure. She is responsible. Your behaviour is causing her a problem she doesn't need. Your subversion of the rules is interfering with the way this woman makes her living. She may secretly admire you. But she cannot let you continue doing things in the way that you want to do them.

In many situations, those who might seek the top job(s) should have disqualified themselves from the role simply by considering the application: power as a motivator is the source of all hypocrisy and should preclude its seeker from their desire. This is not to enter into the fallacy that all bosses are, by definition, awful versions of the human they might have been – in some cases it is their passion and their brilliance that has caused them to have taken on the Lonsdale Belt of leadership (sometimes against their will or judgement) – but it is to establish that hierarchies might be controlled by people who seek to keep things as they are.

In challenging orthodoxies you will be challenging the rule book, which may very well be a puddle of sketched nonsenses, but adherence to which is the credo through which the majority feed their families. (Above all, fear the parent whose livelihood is threatened.) If you poke your finger in things that no one has previously thought to poke their finger in, then expect resistance, expect angered rejection of your ideas, expect the guardians of average to close ranks in order that they might form a wall from which they will combine a coordinated pointing action with the nigh on overt implication that you, you silly maverick, are clearly insane. You must be. You are on your own. You are the only person who thinks this.

Expect also sundry accusations of (mental) disorder. And accept them. Your accusers will be right: mavericks have a disorder, are a disorder (or a desire for it). Maverick nature comes with the dictate that things as they are, in the order in which they are currently arranged, must be altered, must change; things as they are, are failing to do what they are meant to do (or are failing to do what they are meant to do in a sufficiently brilliant, life enhancing or imaginative way), and the world as it is, and the structures as they are, cannot continue with the delusion that they can't be improved by being exploded.

It is disordered thinking, or deliberately considering how you might actively disorder things, that causes the big changes. Someone first had to pick up the ball and think, 'Hell, what is the worst that could happen?' for the near global religion of rugby to have been born. Someone had to wonder if, rather than letting a vinyl record run, as it always previously had, in a clockwise manner, what would happen if it was run, repetitively, back and forth under the stylus? It was this abrasive and unconventional act that tore up the idea that to be a musician you had to learn a musical instrument, and which gave birth to hip hop: the most democratic art form since punk, and a media through which many a disenfranchised young human has found a voice.

So what, in the positive sense of the word, characterises the maverick? What are you, reader, other than just the accused? Let us put you under the microscope. Chiefly, you will have had a lifetime's commitment to questioning accepted truths; to deciding that if everyone is going south for the winter, then the only morally acceptable path, clearly, is to go north; from a developed understanding that the world of organised commerce (for which read also most political systems) seeks little more than to divide the world into dauphins and paupers, and to profit from this division. A maverick rejects. A maverick rejects the 'truths' that exist in order to condemn them and their families to versions of slavery; a maverick rejects the idea that convention is of any value for anyone other than those who impose the ideas of what is acceptable in order that they might profit from them; and a maverick rejects mass (or elite ideas inflicted on the masses as a means of asserting intellectual dominance) ideas of taste. A maverick understands that the very idea of 'taste' is merely a means of the castes with a vested interest in keeping things as they are asserting the idea of the slave caste being less intelligent than their slavers, as they are unable to commune with (or afford) the slavers' 'taste' in culture, furniture and garments.

But a maverick does not only reject. There is little point in being the impotent cynic putrefying slowly in the corner of a room which no one wants to enter. To inhabit this position is to inhabit the slow death of everything precious. A maverick is not defined by the number of times they say no; a maverick is defined by the number of alternative realities they are able to create. Constructing these alternative realities is what is called your work. And you must be devoted to it if you are to win.

This is an excerpt from the introduction of Phil Beadle's current work in progress, *Rules for Mavericks: How to Lead Life as a 'Creative Visionary Iconoclast' and Still Pay the Rent*, to be published by Crown House Publishing in 2016.

Notes
1   This adjective has always struck the author as telling.
2   A word on job titles. For those who profit from institutional life, the job title is the external expression of the ego. If a hugely mediocre person is called a director in their daily life, it will give them a sense of importance that they will carry into places where it is entirely ridiculous. They will say, 'Don't you know who I am?' to waiters when they are merely the assistant director of a suburban

stationers. Beware your dealings with these people. The fact that you are not deferent to, or even remotely interested in, the status their job title affords them will offend them.

3   Nor by studying the minutiae of that tradition to see if it is flawed and whether she can improve on it.

Chapter 11

Knowing Your Students Beyond the Data

On Values, Valuing and Saying Hello

Crista Hazell

Relationships are complex, multifaceted things that take hard work, time, compassion, dedication and love – this we know. Relationships with students are just as demanding. How often do we find ourselves saying, 'What's the point?', as yet again our professional care and support is thrown back at us. Well, there absolutely *is* a point and our reactions are just as important as our actions in demonstrating the extent to which we value the young people with whom we are working. Which means, at times, we have to work harder than ever to make sure that we value all those who cross our paths, and in big ways as well as more subtle ones.

Everyone needs to feel valued. It is one of life's basic needs. If we are noticed and acknowledged, praised and rewarded, then we grow, we develop, we, dare I say it, soften a little. The barriers come down and we start to show increasingly more of ourselves. It is the same for students as it is for teachers. We all want to be accepted and respected but, as the professionals in the room, often we need to make the first move and ensure that we find the time, despite ever increasing workloads, to reach out to our learners and make a connection directly with them. Every school day we must build and maintain a bridge to our students, not to mention to the colleagues we work alongside.

The good news here is that little things count in a big way. The smallest of positive comments. A handwritten sticky note. Noticing and sharing your delight at their presence. Highlighting the progress they have made since the previous lesson. Each act strengthens this connection. It shows the children in your room that they are valued, their contributions matter and their effort is appreciated. Most importantly it shows we value them enough to care. It is a process that starts the moment the students arrive at the classroom door, positively acknowledging them with a non-verbal cue such as a smile, a nod or a wink, along with a verbal cue expressing pleasure at seeing them.

It doesn't take long but it matters if you want to build a relationship with them and create a positive tone for the session. Your mission is to welcome students into the learning space so they feel happy and fully aware that any and all positive contributions are listened to, respected and recognised. Quality learning experiences involve challenges of increasing complexity, both individually and as a group. This is something that can only be successfully approached when the students are ready for action emotionally as well as physically and when they are truly on board with you. For example, in my context, teaching modern foreign languages, we are developing language usage whilst also improving pronunciation, competence and confidence along the way. It is what we do. But if the climate isn't right for learning, because they don't feel valued, then the hoped for progress will not be forthcoming.

Taking the time to get to know your students beyond the data is crucial and, curiously, is a key element to making progress and improving the data. Knowing your learners creates warmth and trust and shows you are interested in them as human beings and not as numbers, target levels or grades. It allows more opportunities for flexibility in your lessons, for learning off-piste, for making the learning experience flexible and responsive, never straitjacketed by an impersonal lesson plan. Discovering details about their daily lives and challenges, their family and friends, their likes, loves and dislikes as well as their achievements outside of school, all in order to support them along their learning journey, will pay dividends in terms of their learning, risk taking and progress as well as vastly improving your relationship with them. It takes time and commitment but this is a small price to pay for the returns you will more often than not get back.

And how do you get to know this information? Talk to them! Simple as that. Make sure you build time into your lessons, meetings and activities to chat to them about them. Always acknowledge students in the corridors and snatch a quick conversation with them. Treating them with absolute positivity from the moment they enter your space until the second they leave is paramount. Showering them with affection, encouragement and the basic premise that you will never give up on them cannot fail to encourage even the most reticent teenage linguist to have a go and eventually to build up the confidence to always do their best. Sometimes they even do it with a smile, and if you are really lucky they might volunteer!

What's more, remember that sharing is caring. Sharing a little bit of *you* makes the learning journey fun and deepens the bond of trust. It proves that we are human too, leading real lives and not just rolling out a sleeping bag at the end of the school day once they have all left the premises.

Of course, there will be times when things don't go to plan and situations arise that, despite our best efforts, necessitate consequences and negative repercussions such as punishments or a temporary dismissal from the learning space and the group. What is important here is to *never* hold a grudge. It is not the weak teacher who forgives her miscreant students but the strong one. Always smiling, always doing your utmost to be positive, always giving the appearance that you actually like them, this all allows students to accept this norm and, in turn, supports and encourages them to do their best, nearly always.

This may seem a daunting task day in, day out, especially on a rainy Friday last period, but this is the time when it matters the most. The impact upon student behaviour, their attitude to learning and focus both in your classroom and across your department is phenomenal, not to mention a serious reduction in things being thrown back at you – both physically and metaphorically.

Valuing students costs nothing other than the time it takes to get to know them and then maintain that connection on a daily basis. As 99% of you reading this will know, learning a language is hard. Confidence is key here and having a go is more important than being perfect. The 'show me what you know' approach (as opposed to the 'let me show you what you don't know' approach so often used in schools) is superb for supporting creativity in all contexts and has learners falling over themselves to show off their flair, originality and new found skills. You will be surprised by the sheer level of student desire to be amazing and original. It is truly a joy to bear witness to their achievements and celebrate their successes, and creating the right conditions at an emotional level from the outset means they start to forget how difficult learning a language is and actually enjoy rising to the challenge, despite themselves.

A word of warning: if your body language, the tone of your voice and the previous experience your students have had in your lessons are not congruent with your message, it will not work. It is not what you do, it is what they think that counts. Quite honestly, students are incredible readers of emotion and their empathy meters are alarmingly accurate. Which means you must truly feel open to their presence in order for them to respond to the risks you wish them to take. The minute you truly believe you are willing for them to take risks is the minute they will start taking them. So, wear your values – and the fact that you value them – on your sleeve. Consistently mind your language, both verbal and non-verbal, constantly wear a smile, choose unconditional positive regard to all students unremittingly and watch them blossom. *Bonne chance!*

Recommended video:

Rita Pierson, 'Every Kid Needs A Champion' (May 2013). Available at: https://www.ted.com/talks/rita_pierson_every_kid_needs_a_champion?language=en

Chapter 12

Grow Your Own Cabinet of Curiosities

An Inventory of Exhibits To Get You
Started On the Road To Wonder

Dr Matthew McFall

St Augustine wrote, 'The reward of patience is patience.' The same can be said of wonder. The more you wonder the more you see wonder. And the more wondrous the world becomes.

Moments of wonder are rooted in interest and there are all sorts of beneficial and enlivening things that make up a potential wonder. There are the fruitful dimensions of novelty, mystery and surprise, amongst others. Bearing these positives in mind, we might expect to witness and experience all sorts of desirable effects arising from people wondering: joy, meaningfulness, curiosity, willingness to discover and learn. All meeting in what those nice positive psychologists refer to as eudemonia: a happy soul.

But how do we get to the treasure? Well, you need a little time and space to dedicate, a cheerful intention to share and celebrate a curio or three with others and an ever vigilant eye, for you never know when you will next stumble upon something perfectly wondrous. After all, the world is full of marvels if we have the eyes to see them and the desire to look for them. There is wonder alike in prisms, telephones, fruit flies and lumps of coal. But most important of all is the opportunity to *encounter* these objects and artefacts – and help others do the same.

A Cabinet of Curiosities, a venerable tradition with a rich history, is one way of helping to provide direct experiences of all things wondrous.

A Cabinet can be a room, a shed, a caravan … The schools and institutions I have the pleasure of working with have no end of practical and inspiring ingenuity when it comes to making a space for wonder. If you do not have a room, a cupboard will be admirable, but so will a shelf or a box. Even a matchbox is big enough to hold a piece of awesomeness. The old school tradition of the nature table deserves a comeback, and augmented with ingenious constructions (a painting, a puzzle, a planisphere) and you have a microcosm of marvels.

Having established your Cabinet, let others in to see it and simply have a decent conversation. In my experience, your wonder space will grow, like an analogue wiki, as others add first their thoughts and then start to tentatively proffer their own items of wonder for exhibition. 'Sir, I found this and I was wondering …' Establish this sort of dedicated space in a school, for example, and imagine how, with a lightness of touch and a commitment to proper shared ownership, the wonders – and wonder – will increase.

What I present to you here is a simple Inventory of Exhibits that will serve you and yours well when you set out to establish your own wonder space. It will be a good companion on your next treasure hunt, whether trawling charity shops, crawling through your attic or clicking your way through the Internet (surely the vastest Cabinet of Curiosities the universe has ever known). The list is, of course, a work in progress, but represents a feast of delights for head, hand and heart.

The important thing is to start small and watch it grow. You need only the commitment to making some dedicated space for sharing and then allowing things to propagate. People sharing, admiring, smiling, exclaiming together – that's a vision of achievable wonder.

May your wonders never cease.

Mealworms Pupae Jumping beans Stick insects	*Mimosa pudica* (sensitive plant) Resurrection plants Air plants Moss Artichokes Sunflower heads Gunnera leaves Seeds (banana, bird of paradise, acorn, coconut, assorted trees) Galls	Teeth (human, horse) Bones (vertebrae) Skulls (inc. models) Fossils (megalodon, ammonite, mammoth rib)	Feathers Eggs (ostrich, replicas) Incubators Bird song recordings Abandoned nests
Spider skin Dead bees Wasp nests			
Sea monkeys Triops		Shells Mermaid's purses Goose barnacles Echinoderms Crabs	
Parasites			
Slime moulds	Celeriac Voodoo lily Valerian root Carbolic soap Durian fruit Vanilla pods Scents (uncommon)	Models and charts of: The brain The skull The spine The alimentary canal Glass eye	Fool's gold Coal Geodes Gold Carbon Hydrogen/tritium Mercury Nitinol Polymers

Two-piece puzzles Robust puzzle boxes Trick padlocks Word safes Tangrams Soma cubes Tower of Hanoi Marble solitaire		Periodic tables Composition of the human body Maps Gall–Peters projection map Globe of the world Charts	Clockwork mechanisms Clocks Cat's whisker detector Telegraphs Morse transmitters Typewriters Telephones
	Magnets		Cabinet cards Postcards Old newspapers/periodicals Old catalogues
Jacob's ladder Handheld dexterity devices Trammel of Archimedes Bilboquet Yo-yo Cat's cradle	Crooke's radiometer Benham disk Euler's disk Tippe top	Labyrinths Mazes	Dictionaries (OED, Blackie, Chambers, Malay, Esperanto) Riddles Jokes Secret codes

Dobble Oska Quoridor Quarto Marbles Jacks Dice	Scribbling top Levitating top Rattlebacks/celts Thaumatropes	[Space for missing wonders]	Cuneiform Shorthand Game books *Thunks* (Gilbert) *Awe & Wonder* (McFall) *Natural History Book* (DK)
Möbius strip Klein bottle	Origami Hexaflexagons Fortune Teller 'Fortune telling fish'	Masks Wooden headrests	Boxes Button tins French knitting
Conjuring sets Ropes and knots Calculator cards Magic compasses	Optical illusions Magic Eye autostereograms Anamorphosis Kinetic illusions	Oracles Fortune cookies Dispensers Questions Words	A Museum of Boring Things Miniature Cabinets of Curiosities

Recommended book:

Lawrence Weschler, *Mr Wilson's Cabinet of Wonder: Pronged Ants, Horned Humans, Mice on Toast, and other Marvels of Jurassic Technology* (London: Vintage, 1996)

Chapter 13

Complex Doesn't Have To Be Complicated

How To Cope With Complexity Without Becoming a Simpleton

Dr Debra Kidd

I have some sympathy with the 'what works' agenda. It seems to me that every day I wander around my house kicking one appliance or another and shouting, 'Why won't you work?' As soon as I get one thing fixed another one breaks down. Education is not so different. You spend a lot of money 'fixing' one aspect, but not only does it fail to reap the rewards you expected but something else goes wrong as well. You put in one measure, like league tables, and it has an unintended consequence, such as inflating local house prices. Life is like those games at fairgrounds – the ones where you bop a frog on the head. You hit one and another pops up somewhere else. If only we could be in control. If only we could be certain of 'what works'.

Talking of unintended consequences and unexpected frogs, there has been much written about 'complex adaptive systems' in the classroom. These are systems in which there is 'emergence'; that is to say, where the outcome is greater than the sum of its parts. In their research into what makes great teaching, Coe et al. accepted that while they had compiled a list of six qualities that seemed to make a difference, they had to accept that there was an ephemeral quality to being a great teacher, something the research can't quite pinpoint, that made it emergent.[1] In short, we can tick off the attributes a good teacher should have and the actions a good teacher should do but, at the end of the day, we cannot *guarantee* that any of it will work. There is something other – an X factor or secret ingredient – that happens in the relationship between teacher and pupil which makes for really great learning. And it can't be ranked in a list.

The Dutch educational philosopher Gert Biesta warns that in attempting to reduce and mitigate complexity, we run the risk of damaging the system we are trying to enhance – and with alarming consequences. He suggests that we reach a point of simplistic thinking 'where complexity reduction turns into unjustifiable and uneducational suppression and where suppression becomes oppression'.[2] It seems to me that in our quest for certainty – a quest that has been taking place since Labour's 'Education, Education, Education' election victory in 1997 – we have, in fact, created new and unforeseen problems that are more and more difficult to solve. We bash one frog and another pops up.

It's easy to write in abstract terms, but let's look at one example as a case study of how badly we can get something wrong when we reduce and simplify, when we shine a beam of truth onto one aspect of a problem and immediately plunge others into darkness.

Phlippin' phonics

Our current Year 7s are the Phonic Boom generation. They are the first group of children for whom there has been an expectation throughout the whole of their education that they will have been taught to read using synthetic phonics. Of course, older children would have also been given a precautionary dose of phonics – those working in secondary education will have seen Year 7s coming through over the past two or three years who have been taught phonics, but the current generation is the 'all through from reception class' group. You would expect, given the heralding of phonics as the silver bullet answer to literacy problems in this country, that last year's SATs results would have shown a huge improvement. In actual fact, there was a modest 3% increase in reading scores, which is, of course, to be welcomed, but is hardly dramatic. Nevertheless, 89% of our children are leaving primary school at the expected standard. When you account for special educational needs and second language speakers, that's not a bad picture at all. Certainly not the pessimistic picture we see in the media.

But let's look a little more distantly at the bigger picture. SATs do not form the end point of our education system. We need to zoom out in order to get a better picture, and if we do this we see some worrying gaps in our thinking.

In their analysis of the impact of the teaching of synthetic phonics across Clackmannanshire, Johnston and Watson concluded that 'the synthetic phonics approach as part of the reading curriculum, is more effective than the analytic phonics approach'.[3] The findings of this report led to the Rose Review into literacy in England and a push for synthetic phonics in all primary schools from the Labour government.[4] Initial teacher training provision was inspected carefully to ensure that student teachers were receiving training in synthetic phonics and this focus continued with the new coalition government in 2010.

In universities across the land, units on children's literature and reading for pleasure made way for phonics. And the coalition did something that no government has ever done before – they made a pedagogy statutory. It is now law that all pupils will study synthetic phonics. There is even a test with nonsense words on it. What seemed like an effective intervention very quickly became a form of oppression.

But what was largely ignored throughout all of this was the caveat that Johnston and Watson included in their report: 'although the boys read better than the girls [as a result of the teaching of synthetic phonics], they nevertheless reported a less favourable attitude to reading'.[5] In short, boys were technically improving their reading but showing less enjoyment in the process. This was a finding supported by the OECD: 'although most pupils in England are competent readers by secondary age, their "interest and commitment" to reading is declining "substantially"'.[6]

And while boys were seen to be closing the reading gap with girls in primary school as a result of synthetic phonics, the gains were lost at secondary: the gap in reading test scored between genders aged 7 is 7%, by the age of 16, this has doubled to 14%.[7] It would seem that learning to decode and encode alone is not enough to sustain interest in reading for boys, and this matters in the long term. Sullivan and Brown's research for the Institute of Education shows that between the ages of 10 and 16, children who read for pleasure more than once a week gain higher results in tests (even in maths) than those who do not. Children who performed at the same level for reading at the ages of 5 and 10 were polarised by the age of 16 as they did not read for pleasure. It is therefore hugely important that children leaving primary school are not simply technically competent at reading, but are enthusiastic.[8]

If we step back and look at the whole complex picture, we see that it is, in fact, the habit of reading *regularly and for pleasure* that makes the most difference for most children. So surely we need to ask whether or not it has been wise to focus so relentlessly on one single solution in primary school without considering the wider picture – a question that the coalition government began belatedly asking, but not really communicating to schools.[9] In order to do this, the government need to do more than commission reports. They need to look closely at the impact that phonics and SATs tests have on children's *appetite* for reading.

It would be wrong to say that we should abandon phonics and focus instead on reading for pleasure. All this would do is shine the 'light of truth' – and the shadows that throws – somewhere else. But what we could do is illuminate the whole picture. To do so is complex but not complicated. Phonics takes 20 minutes a day. The rest of the time should be filled with the awe, wonder and beauty of text. Reading should be associated, for example, with comfort. How many of us read at a desk for pleasure? Instead, we snuggle to read. Reading should also be associated with friendships and communities. Children love to talk about their favourite characters and books – we all do in fact – hence the explosion of book clubs around the country. If we can put these things in place, alongside the other, more technical elements, we might just have the conditions in place to make our children better readers. Not just in order to pass tests, but to enrich and enhance their lives in a way that only reading can.

Recommended book:

Gert J. J. Biesta, *The Beautiful Risk of Education* (Boulder, CO: Paradigm, 2013)

Notes

1   R. Coe, C. Aloisi, S. Higgins and L. E. Major, *What Makes Great Teaching? Review of the Underpinning Research* (London: Sutton Trust, 2014). Available at: http://www.suttontrust.com/researcharchive/great-teaching/.

2   G. J. J. Biesta, *The Beautiful Risk of Education* (Boulder, CO: Paradigm, 2013), p. 2.

3   R. Johnston and J. Watson, *The Effects of Synthetic Phonics Teaching On Reading and Spelling Attainment: A Seven Year Longitudinal Study* (Edinburgh: Scottish Executive, 2005). Available at: http://www.scotland.gov.uk/Resource/Doc/36496/0023582.pdf, p. 9.

4   J. Rose, *Independent Review of the Teaching of Early Reading: Final Report* [Rose Review] (Nottingham: DfES, 2006).

5   Johnston and Watson, *The Effects of Synthetic Phonics Teaching*, p. 8.

6   OECD, *PISA 2009 Results: What Students Know and Can Do. Student Performance In Reading, Mathematics and Science (Volume I)* (OECD: Paris, 2010). Available at: http://www.oecd-ilibrary.org/education/pisa-2009-results-what-students-know-and-can-do_9789264091450-en.

7   See National Literacy Trust, *Boys' Reading Commission Report* (London: National Literacy Trust, 2012). Available at: http://www.literacytrust.org.uk/assets/0001/4056/Boys_Commission_Report.pdf, p. 6.

8   A. Sullivan and M. Brown, *Social Inequalities in Cognitive Scores at Age 16: The Role of Reading*, CLS Working Paper 2013/10 (London: Centre for Longitudinal Studies, 2013).

9   Department for Education, Research Evidence on Reading for Pleasure (May 2012). Available at: https://www.gov.uk/government/uploads/system/uploads/attachment_data/file/284286/reading_for_pleasure.pdf.

Chapter 14

Planting Seeds of Aspiration In Schools

The Power Teachers Have To Change Lives

Jim Roberson

Don't just tell me more

Show me more

Let me see more

Help me aspire to be

More.

I'm one of the lucky ones. My teachers didn't just teach me. My coaches didn't just coach me. Anyone can do that. Just go through the motions. Do the bare minimum. Do the day job. Collect their wages at the end of the week. All the time failing to see the adult in the child. What the teachers and the coaches in my life did was more than that. They saw beyond what I was to what I could be – regardless of what that was. And they helped this boy see beyond that too, beyond the environment I grew up in, beyond everything I had experienced to that point. Beyond any self-imposed limitations.

What they did was plant seeds of aspiration.

And, man, do I thank them for that.

For me it started with my parents.

And I thank them for that.

My dad would take the whole family to the Apollo Theater in Harlem. If you know anything about black music, you'll know about that theatre. Anyone who was anyone played there, and I've seen them all – The Temptations, The Jackson 5, Diana Ross, James Brown – the Godfather of Soul.

When you're a young boy with your father watching people like that, people that good, people who looked and spoke like me, that's what plants seeds. Seeds of aspiration. If they can be somebody, I can be somebody.

I thank them all for that.

If you've read my book, *The Discipline Coach*, you'll know Miss Potts. She took us on a school trip to Albany, NY. I was in Year 5. I was about 9. I was on a plane. Seed planted.

Thank you Miss Potts.

I remember my first time being shown (different from 'seeing') the Empire State Building. Wow. The Statue of Liberty. The Bronx Zoo. The Rockefeller Center. Radio City Music Hall. Grand Central Station. The World Trade Center towers. The United Nations headquarters. All on school trips. That's a lot of seeds planted.

So, now, I plant seeds. Every day.

Over the last few years I have taken over 400 young people from England to New York. These kids had barely crossed town before, let alone the Atlantic. We go to the same places. The Empire State Building. Wow. The Statue of Liberty. The space where the World Trade Center towers were. I show them. I teach them to look. I show them other possibilities.

I am a sower of seeds of aspiration.

Good schools do that too. And when I say 'good schools', I don't give a damn about what Ofsted think of them. I mean good schools. Schools that look at their children, see beyond what they see and see something different. Something special. And get their children to see that too.

In good schools, teachers look at their students, their neighbourhood, their parents, themselves. And then they see what else can be done.

Planting seeds is not about quick wins. They take a lifetime to flourish. I work with a lot of young people who fit the 'pupil premium' bill. I tell schools to look at these children and think about the qualities they will need to achieve, to be someone, to count. You can't break a cycle without looking beyond what's there. Thinking differently. Thinking about different possibilities. Sowing seeds of what else it could be like, all of it.

I call it the 'driver' state of mind. New expectations. New aspirations. Not the passenger any more. In the driving seat now.

And there was the Work Appreciation Programme.

Motive: Teach students the values involved in working. The benefits involved in working. Not benefits instead of working.

Process: Four weeks of summer holiday. Four weeks of their time. Their investment in themselves. We found them placements in places like IBM, Zurich, P&O Ferries. They worked, real work, for 24 hours a week. They weren't at school but they were learning. Learning to work. Learning that people could have expectations of them, that one day this could be their life if they chose it.

Seeds of aspiration are also seeds of choice.

Each one had to achieve a minimum of 95% attendance to be eligible. But we aimed for 100%. We got them bank accounts. They earned a salary of £59 a week. Their money, earned money. It was paid into their account every Friday for four weeks. They had debit cards so they could take their money out if they chose to.

So many seeds. How to budget. How to spend wisely. How to look after your money. How to look after yourself. How to get up, get dressed, get there on time and get the job done. Some had never witnessed that. But unemployment doesn't have to be hereditary, not if we can show them a different reality. See beyond and plant the seeds that will help them get there.

And seeds can be planted constantly. The trip to the airport and looking at the different careers they can see. The trip to local sites of interest such as the police station or the fire station.

Seeds of aspiration flourish, and disaffection finds it hard to take root.

What seeds are you planting? And I mean beyond just 'doing your job'. Yes, I know we have issues with staffing for trips, with budgets, with willpower. But spread your net further. Get more people DBS checked (formerly CRB) and use them to plant seeds with you. We have used community workers and the police. It helps to develop healthy relationships.

Get yourself in front of parents in person. Not an e-mail or a letter or a phone call. Face to face. And ask them to come in. Parents helping out the dinner ladies, the lollipop man, being seen, building relationships. Modelling to young people how grown-ups operate. Being polite. Communicating well. Being sociable and respectful. Learning how to conduct yourself in public.

For everything we teach there is a place we can visit to bring the subject to life and plant seeds of aspiration as we do so. If you want me to learn French or German, take me to France or Germany. Make it relevant. Real. And at the same time you are showing me something different. Battlefields, art exhibitions, sporting events, churches, landscapes, castles – they all count. They all contain the possibility of different realities.

And watch out! You never know when and how the seeds you plant will reappear bearing fruit. I was recently at an Independent Thinking Big Day Out in Epsom when I came across a former student of mine. He had been on my New York trip several years ago. A friend and he were into guitars, so I took them to a Fender guitar shop in Manhattan. They each had a guitar made. We shared this with the audience. He remembered every detail, even though it was over 20 years ago.

Seeds of aspirations can provide real and lasting relevance to education. These seeds grow and have an impact on the lives of young people throughout their lives. And they learn to plant seeds too.

This young man is now a teacher. He runs trips to New York every year.

Recommended book:

Denzel Washington, *A Hand To Guide Me* (Des Moines, IA: Meredith Books, 2007)

Chapter 15

There Isn't an App For That

Jazz, Flow and Thirsty Learners

Mark Anderson

Want blended learning?

Trying to get your R on SAMR?

Thinking about packing up your TPACK?

Need your mindset to grow?

Teaching with technology isn't just about the tech. Technology is there to serve us, aid us and, in some cases, guide us. It is also there to enable us to capitalise on the learning potential of the young people we are so lucky to work with. The problems come when others – that is to say teachers and senior leaders – see the procurement of technology as being of itself the saviour of education. There is a real need to engage with creative thinking when it comes to learning, particularly when looking at the use of technology and its place in learning. Simply put – it isn't the panacea many people think it is. Raising achievement with technology does not end with the commissioning of a purchase order for new equipment. Before we start filling our schools with hardware, the strategy for learning needs to be right. And there's no app for that.

If we are going to get the best from our students, whether it be encouraging and exploiting a curiosity for learning, developing the real grit and determination they need to succeed, encouraging the ability to be truly creative or the bravery to try out new things and discover what the world looks like through different eyes, then knowing how to bring out the best in our learners is paramount. Yes, a partnership with technology can go a long way. But, technology doesn't have all the answers all of the time, despite the impression given by our friends at Google!

It is important to remember that, unlike in the good old days, technology changes and develops on a daily basis. Literally. There is simply no way that we can keep up with it all. There is a way, however, that we can master it.

I have written previously about how important it is to remember that teachers are the masters of pedagogy and students are the masters of technology. While this is true to a certain extent (and I still feel that saying 'I'm not good with computers' is simply not good enough) we need to be looking for ways that we can bring together both elements of mastery to encourage our students to greater heights. And push ourselves to be better at both pedagogy and technology at the same time.

So, what does mastery in digital learning entail? When I consider this conundrum I often think about the 'greats' in life, those people who are able to do things that beggar belief. When you witness the most amazing people in action, they give us moments of awe and wonder that make us ask, how do they do it? How does one individual create such brilliance? How did they get to be this good?

Professional skateboarders are a great example of how far the human body can be stretched to achieve incredible feats. In his PopTech talk from 2013, Rodney Mullen explains what it is like to be a professional skateboarder and the effort required to perform some of the astonishing tricks.[1] What it boils down to is hours of failure, hours of falling over and picking yourself back up again, trying again and again and again, relentlessly improving bit by bit, one bruise at a time.

Whether it's a world class sportsman like Mullen or world class artist like Jacqueline du Pré, playing her cello with apparent ease and sublime perfection, what we are looking at is what is known as 'flow', a concept highlighted in the pioneering work of Mihaly Csikszentmihalyi. It's something you can even observe in this video of a 4-year-old playing the piano.[2]

We can also observe this important state when we look at young people playing games on their game consoles or hand-held devices. And remember, these are the same children who can't seem to focus in your lesson for more than a few minutes. Game developers look to engage their players in this state of flow. As you can see in this diagram adapted from game designer Noah Falstein, the optimum state of game flow occurs at the point where there is a balance between the complexity of the game and the ease with which the various tasks are completed.

It is an area known as the 'sweet spot', and it is not a single point but something that evolves as the skill level of the player improves. As you are stretched and challenged within the game, as you face new situations and gain new skills, you are pushed to achieve increasingly difficult tasks. In other words, the more you are pushed to learn and grow, the more you are taken to higher and higher levels. And if you stay in the sweet spot, you don't even notice what's happening. That's flow.

In computer games we see a continual increase in the level of challenge offered combined with frequent failure, which is part of the learning process, and a focus on intrinsic motivation to push the gamer ever onward. The gamers are refining and improving their technique all the time, using

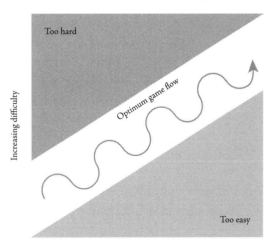

A better flow. Adapted from Noah Falstein

failure as feedback to develop their skills. All the time there is high challenge, and nothing is too easy.

As master practitioners in the classroom we can instil these skills in our learners. Constructing learning challenges that are high on challenge, low on stress and where there are opportunities for constructive failure, all contribute to a great learning experience. Learning activities should be crafted to be not too difficult, but also not too easy. Remember, you're aiming for the sweet spot. It's the same for you as you develop your technological skills. Engage your brain by using skills you've picked up previously, start with what you know and where you are at, but then kick-start your creative brain with play, trial and error, failure as feedback, challenge and enjoyment, and then you will find yourself using technology you've never used before and in ways that will surprise you.

Jazz musician Miles Davis said, 'Play what you know and then play above what you know'. Be comfortable where you start but always stretch yourself. It's called 'playing around', or in some cases 'noodling'. It's the same with the skateboarders, the gamers, the sports professionals – and the children in your classroom.

To do this we also need to instil resilience in our learners in such a way that it isn't lost as they get older. And one of the ways we can do this is to develop it in ourselves too. As professionals, by deliberately playing, starting with the knowledge we already have, by implementing strategies that we know work for us and finely tuning these, by stretching ourselves with new strategies until we fail, by demonstrating the resilience to pick ourselves back up again and by trying again, we can take things to the next level. Play what you know and then play above what you know.

Instil this in your learners and they will always have a thirst for learning and discovery. And you know what, there isn't an app for that.

Recommended book:

Jane McGonigal, *Reality is Broken: Why Games Make Us Better and How They Can Change the World* (London: Vintage, 2012)

Notes

1   R. Mullen, Getting Back Up [video] (2013). Available at: http://poptech.org/popcasts/rodney_mullen_getting_back_up.

2   See https://www.youtube.com/watch?v=omuYi2Vhgjo.

Chapter 16

Athena Versus the Machine

Values Led Leadership In a Time of Change

Martin Robinson

If I had to live my life again, I would have made a rule to read some poetry and listen to some music at least once every week; for perhaps the parts of my brain now atrophied would thus have been kept active through use. The loss of these tastes is a loss of happiness, and may possibly be injurious to the intellect, and more probably to the moral character, by enfeebling the emotional part of our nature.

Charles Darwin, *Autobiography*

Imagine.

The comp down the road from you is changing. It has to change because it is such a crap school. Apparently … Apparently there's a new head teacher. Out with the old and in with the new. The school has changed its name, its building, it's now an academy, it has changed its uniform – new boots and panties. It wants to change its kids, make them more aspirational. It wants to change its kids' parents too, make them take an interest, make them aspirational too. It's in the process of driving out old, decrepit, useless staff and bringing in new, young, dynamic staff – singletons with their future ahead of them.

There are new targets. New initiatives. New exam results. And you knew it would work … You can't stop progress. This is the 21st century. Old superstitions replaced by new certainties.

Science united with business values. Look at our mission statement and the values on our lanyards. New values. 'I'm looking for one new value, but nothing comes my way' sang Iggy Pop. Can one ever have 'new values'? If you can jettison old values so easily, what is to say you won't jettison your new ones just as easily?

As Groucho Marx nearly said, 'These are my values, and if you don't like them, I've got others.' Values are principles, morals, standards. We pass them on because they matter. If everything is changing, including values, then you have no values. But you do have anarchy when you disrupt the culture. How does the new regime cope with this? They bring in the terror. They impose their new values by disrupting their new values.

Imagine.

On 14 July 1789, the Storming of the Bastille ... You are in England listening to the leader of the Whig Party, Charles James Fox, saying of the French Revolution, 'How much the greatest event it is that ever happened in the world, and how much the best!' Thomas Paine was encouraged by the idea of establishing a new French identity from scratch, based on better principles and new ways of organising the nation. This was to be the Enlightenment personified, the rational over the traditional. As Paine wrote in *Common Sense*, sometime before the French Revolution, 'We have it in our power to begin the world over again.'

We need change, so let's start again! And it's completely right-headed, of course. Our structures, everything that is in our dominion in a school, are man-made. We made them, and like a child with a lot of wooden blocks, it can be great fun to knock them all down and start again. The progressive change-maker realises the arbitrary nature of our stories, that things don't have to be this way ... We need 21st century skills, we need 21st century institutions, we need kids to be trained for the future. Capitalism where 'all that is solid melts into air' is fetishised.

The utilitarian view says that we need 21st century skills for jobs that, bizarrely, don't yet exist. Who knows what jobs will be needed in the future? There might be some great global calamity and we wake up from disaster in a post-technological age needing to return to the skills of our ancestors. The Scouts are no longer learning how to tie knots – I mean, what is the point?! Certain crafts are becoming very rare. Thatchers (I use that word with great sensitivity), stonemasons, bookbinders – these are dying crafts no longer needed in our concrete, kindled age. How many crafts are becoming extinct? How many of us children know how to do what our parents could do? But forget the past! Everything has changed – we need to harness the technical know-how of the computer age. Bliss that it is in this dawn to be alive!

We are all futurologists now.

Edmund Burke put it this way: 'You began by despising everything that belonged to you.' He went on to describe how the old ways had faults, but, within their ways, are the seeds of improvement: 'Respecting your forefathers, you would have been taught to respect yourselves.'

Thomas Paine thought we should replace the wrong of the past with right. He insisted that the forces of tradition, the old regime, 'tremble at the approach of principles, and dread the precedent that threatens their overthrow'. And this is powerful. If the past is wrong then we need to ensure that the future is right. Paine pitches thought against tradition: 'I scarcely ever quote; the reason is, I always think.' Oh, the paradox: he makes an appeal to principles, rather than precedent, as his values are about change.

Paine argues too for a scientific, individual liberalism, against Burke's authority laden habit and traditionalism. For Paine, reason stands as a beacon against ignorance. He says about the founding of 'America': 'by the simple operation of constructing government on the principles of society and the rights of man, every difficulty retires, and all parts are brought into cordial unison. There, the poor are not oppressed, the rich are not privileged … and as there is nothing to render them wretched, there is nothing to engender riots and tumults.' Yes, this is the problem: the continuous thrust into the golden future is uncertain. We think we have the answer, we think we know what we are changing things for, but we really don't. Nowadays, 'the market' becomes the justification for all sorts of crimes against learning perpetrated on unfulfilled school kids. There are some progressives who just want to reject all that is old because it is old. This is not education; it is euthanasia.

But what if our old school and our *ancien régime* is corrupt or useless? Is that not a reason for tearing it all down? It might indeed be. So many wrong turns might have been made, but just think for a moment what message this sends out – when we have made a mess of things we must destroy the past. We should forget our identity and like a notorious prisoner on release we need to have a new identity forged for us. We know the past contains mistakes and accidents, but so too will the future. As G. K. Chesterton wrote: 'The whole modern world has divided itself into Conservatives and Progressives. The business of Progressives is to go on making mistakes. The business of Conservatives is to prevent mistakes from being corrected.' This is the balance. Education is a place where the generations, past and future, meet. The teacher representing the past meets the pupil who will make the future, and they meet, crucially, in the present.

Some people hate 'education' just because it looks old fashioned. They want to throw technology at it and argue for a future where all teachers have been successfully replaced by hole-in-the-wall machines or computer games that entertain the child by developing her marketable skills. The future deems that we should all be autonomous individuals buffeted by the global utilitarian market and that our schools should train people in these skills. Not values, skills. And in the next 30 years the schools that we currently see, imagine, will be disbanded. In the age of individualism we will have no need for these institutions – we will finally be free! Free from uniformity: no more school, no more teachers, school's out for a permanent summer fed by Wikipedia.

But what is lost? What is lost?

As Keats wrote in 'Ode On a Grecian Urn': '"Beauty is truth, truth beauty," – that is all / Ye know on earth, and all ye need to know.' For Keats: 'Negative Capability, … is when man is capable of being in uncertainties, mysteries, doubts, without any irritable reaching after fact & reason … the sense of Beauty … obliterates all consideration … the willingness to embrace uncertainty, live with mystery, and make peace with ambiguity.' Or, 'The concept of "negative capability" is the ability to contemplate the world without the desire to try and reconcile contradictory aspects or fit it into closed and rational systems.'

The progressive Brazilian philosopher Roberto Unger calls for decentralisation. He wants a revolution in education that privileges cooperation in teaching and learning rather than individualism and authoritarianism. He thinks teaching should be dialectical from at least two points of view, where the mind is both a machine and an anti-machine. The mind has negative capability, and so should our institutions. This way, he believes, change can be substantial but it should be gradualist and experimental. Permanent vanguardist innovation – innovation led by and for the *Übermensch* – excludes most people, whereas Unger believes we need to disseminate the ability to change their circumstances to the very people involved. For Unger, progressives should not be about aiming for some supreme objective of equality, rather they should be looking at raising ordinary humanity to a higher plane of life, of capability, of experience, of scope in the here and now. And in this he is right. We can keep our values by enacting our values, by allowing staff to be the drivers of their lives. The machine of the school needs to free the imaginations of its staff!

Some have tried to deliver a form of freedom to pupils using student voice and child centred learning, but what of freeing the teacher? What if we talked about the importance of 'teacher voice'? The teacher allowed to cooperate and be the purveyor of gradualist and experimental change? Instead of being the problem the teacher might, indeed, be the solution.

And then give staff what they really need: time. Invest in more staff rather than more middle management. Introduce a flatter management structure and trust teachers more. Instead of the latest technology, gathering dust, have more free periods for classroom teachers. Introduce the old Japanese art of lesson study, allowing for the humane, organic growth of staff generated continuing professional development around a simple structure (like the trivium) on which teachers can build their own classroom methodology, informed by research rather than led by it.

The controversial and eccentric scientist James Lovelock talks about the rational and the intuitive sides of science. He argues that we should encompass both the rational and the irrational. One side we can control and explain but the other side is self-regulating and dynamic: it is about humanity itself. If we want a great education we must include this side, not in our calculations but in our ability to embrace its uncertainty and beauty.

What if education, rather than being a problem to solve, was regarded as something living, something, if you like, human? Let us give this type of humane education a reason: the pursuit of wisdom. Let us give her a name: Athena, the goddess of wisdom. And this education, this humane education, is self-regulating and dynamic. It shares this with all living things ... it is consciousness.

The poetic butterfly, Athena, can easily be destroyed by the wheels of the machine. We must not let this happen. We need to use constraints intelligently to nurture the freedom of our staff. We need values based on tradition and we should entertain ideas that can challenge that tradition. Not ideas distorted through the dogma of a grand future but rooted in the relationships which we have in the here and now. Here we are heirs of the past and makers of the future, but we are of the present – in the now, working collegiately in doubt and hope and love.

Imagine.

Recommended book:

Michael Oakeshott, *The Voice of Liberal Learning* (Indianapolis, IN: Liberty Fund, 2001)

Chapter 17

A Genuine Student Voice
Is One That Is Heard

How Powerful Things Happen When Young People Speak Out

Gill Kelly

I raise up my voice – not so I can shout but so that those without a voice can be heard ... we cannot succeed when half of us are held back.

Malala Yousafzai

In 2009, Malala Yousafzai started blogging for the BBC about life in the Swat Valley, in north-west Pakistan, under Taliban rule. She later became a national figure in her country, appearing on television as a spokesperson for girls' education.

In 2012, at the age of 15, Malala was shot by the Taliban while on board a school bus. The gunman reportedly hijacked the bus, threatened to shoot everyone unless she made herself known and then, when she did, shot her in the head and neck.

In 2014, at the age of 17, Malala became the youngest ever recipient of the Nobel Peace Prize.

This incredible young woman is an inspiration to many young people and adults alike for her resilience and courage in the face of adversity. She has become the embodiment of a new generation of student activism, which has led to a growing global awareness of the needs of all young people – especially girls.

Another campaigner closer to home is Fahma Mohamed, a sixth-form student who led the student body of a Bristol charity called Integrate. Her aim was to put pressure on politicians – especially the then Secretary of State for Education, Michael Gove – to put a stop to the practice of female genital mutilation (FGM). She and others wanted schools to teach children about the practice and raise awareness among the wider community in their fight to halt this act of violence on young girls. She became the 'poster girl' of the *Guardian*'s campaign, and Malala Yousafzai got in touch.[1]

Fahma and her group succeeded in getting Michael Gove to come to their school – the school I was principal of at the time – an inner city, multi-racial academy in Bristol. As a result of his visit and his meetings with Fahma and the group, Gove sent a letter to all schools urging them to make students aware of FGM in advance of the summer holidays, or 'cutting season' as it was known. It was a remarkable achievement and a real validation of the power of the student voice managed and supported by the school context.

Now, both Malala and Fahma had very strong moral imperatives to drive their campaigns and in turn their activism. Malala, inspired by her activist-educator father, had her life and her right to an education to protect. Fahma could see the damage that remaining silent on this issue would have on future generations of girls in her local Somali community and beyond.

Knowing how powerful student opinions can be in affecting change – of the issues at stake and of the young people themselves – it is incredible that some educational institutions do not encourage similar actions by their students. And some actively discourage it. Either they don't want to engage in such activities due to it clashing with a school ethos that might be more about the status quo than affecting change, or they are too wrapped up in a 'fixed ability' paradigm that sees them chasing grades at SATs, GCSEs and beyond, as if learning and growth were a single straight line.

It is not as if we have only just discovered the power of student activism and sought to encourage it. Søren Hansen, in his *The Little Red Schoolbook*, was encouraging freedom of expression back in 1971:

> *Truth can be told in many ways. Don't be afraid to tell a teacher about your own attitudes, about what you like, who your friends are, and what sort of problems you have outside school hours. Use the school magazine, the school council, to talk about subjects which you find important. Try to arrange to do an English essay on how you see the school, and use it to write about the most important things, the things you really want to express.*[2]

Hansen goes on to describe the nature of effective student demonstration and protest but only as actions 'after words have failed'. I have heard and experienced both words and actions of protest in my time, with mixed effects.

Of course, I am not advocating student riots, but I am advocating positive, community spirited student action. This socially conscious mindset begins at an early age when parents and family, depending on their context, can inculcate these values in their offspring. Malala's father would let her stay up late to discuss politics in the family home long after her two brothers had gone to bed. However, if such values are not apparent, schools need to engage young learners in discovering and examining what they truly hold dear.

A 'values framework' in the classroom can be used, firstly, to raise awareness of what a community is and, secondly, to help young people identify their place and their role within it. Finding a 'sense of place' – and the sense of belonging that brings – should start at an immediate, local level in a process that should be fun and experiential. Take Year 1 pupils to the local park and museums. Let them make films or audio blogs about their experiences. Get them out and about in what my colleague, Juliet Robertson, so brilliantly describes as 'dirty teaching and learning'.[3]

The older the students are, the more ambitious you can be with the projects. We are all familiar with the Young Enterprise scheme as well as other projects designed to develop entrepreneurial skills in adolescent students. The shift of emphasis I would like to see here is away from the entrepreneur as single minded money-maker and towards a focus on social responsibility through student-led social enterprise projects.

I was inspired by a visit to Detroit in 2012 where I was attending a programme led by the wonderful thinker and writer Margaret Wheatley. As you may know, Detroit is a city that is bankrupt, yet in the midst of this desperation there rose a beacon of hope – the Avalon bakery.[4] What I witnessed was an organisation that took homeless people off the street, gave them a skill they could use, in this case baking, and lent them interest-free capital to get them back on their own feet.

I came back wanting to set up something similar in Bristol, except that these projects would be led by young people.

Any such ambition is fraught with difficulty and, although the steps made are small, three such social enterprises will open for business across the city in 2015. Where they are housed in a school setting they are blended to fit with the post-16 curriculum delivery at level 2. It certainly makes English and Maths GCSE resits a bit more attractive when they take place within a business environment! Another is in a hub situated in the centre of the city where business mentoring will take place. What's more, all of these social enterprises have a sustainable theme – raising awareness and doing something positive about issues such as climate change or using eco-friendly resources such as specially sourced coffee beans.

I am very proud of the students involved in this work. They reassure me that there is more to education than passing exams. Yet none of this is new. Why is it then that not every community has a youth-led social enterprise? Why are we as community leaders in school not doing more to 'activate' children to make a difference on the issues they feel strongly about? To do so would be to transform the relationships in communities as well as raise the profile of effective sustainable education – not to mention creating the next generation of Malalas and Fahmas.

Recommended book:

Malala Yousafzai with Christina Lamb, *I Am Malala: The Girl Who Stood Up for Education and Was Shot by the Taliban* (London: Weidenfeld & Nicolson, 2013)

Notes

1 See A. Topping, Fahma Mohamed: The Shy Campaigner Who Fought for FGM Education, *The Guardian* (28 February 2014). Available at: http://www.theguardian.com/society/2014/feb/28/fahma-mohamed-michael-gove-teach-female-genital-mutilation-class.

2 S. Hansen and J. Jensen, *The Little Red Schoolbook*, tr. B. Thornberry (London: Pinter & Martin, 2014 [1971]), p. 51.

3 J. Robertson, *Dirty Teaching: A Beginner's Guide To Learning Outdoors* (Carmarthen: Independent Thinking Press, 2014).

4 See http://www.avalonbreads.net/welcome/.

Chapter 18

I See No Ships

Visibility and Invisibility In Educational Research

David Cameron

I can barely recall a time when there was such interest in research about, and relevant to, education. Huge attention has been paid to the work of people like John Hattie, Michael Fullan and others, and we have had educational researchers as media stars in the BBC Radio 4 series, *The Educator*.

In the process, we appear to have made neuroscience a veritable battleground for education with a series of genuine – and aspiring – educationalists, going mano-a-mano on the nature of intelligence, the finer points of cognitive science and a range of other issues about 'what works'. In my home patch of Scotland, there has been a long tradition, mainly through the Tapestry Partnership, of bringing together researchers and theorists of international status to talk about their work. Many of them have drawn audiences that filled the Glasgow Concert Hall, with terrific follow-up at local levels.

Elsewhere in the UK, engagement has been just as vibrant and, arguably, more controversial. Social media reverberate with debate about the need for research based practice or evidence led development. Research, however partially used or, in some instances, partially understood, has become the blackjack of educational discourse. It is often wielded to silence opponents rather than stimulate discussion.

The debate, such as it is, seems to accommodate comfortably some very odd dichotomies. Many of those attacking 'progressive' views on the basis of research evidence have been those most contemptuous of 'the Blob' – a group of academics and, er, researchers. What is at play here though is not science but politics. It is an archetypal political tactic to create a powerful enemy that must be slayed in order for progress to be made. This tactic is usually deployed by those in power supported by those with power, a phenomenon brilliantly illustrated in Thomas Frank's book, *What's the Matter With America?*[1] In it, he describes how the Republicans have gained support by opposing a liberal establishment that seems capable of running the country without actually being in power. Like the concept of 'the Blob', such an approach draws on a virulent anti-intellectualism that is the antithesis of a culture that claims to promote research.

Michael Gove, the former secretary of state for education in England, was fond of wielding the research blackjack and was a considerable enthusiast for Blob baiting, a sport without a close season. This made it even more interesting then to read Canadian educational researcher Michael Fullan's account of being invited by the then Labour administration in 2002 to carry out a 'deep audit and assessment of the English Literacy and Numeracy strategies'.[2]

Fullan identified four 'big lessons':

> *Firstly, don't have punitive accountability practices in your systems, they don't work. Secondly, don't become obsessed by targets as this can have more negative impacts. Thirdly, they saw that having a focus on a small number of goals did give the best opportunity to succeed. Finally, they recognised that capacity building amongst leaders and teachers was crucial to development of schools.*

Clearly, neither the government which commissioned the work, nor Mr Gove and the subsequent administration, saw fit to implement these recommendations. Rather, improvement has been sought, to a significant extent, by addressing governance arrangements for schools. I also think it would be fair to argue that targets have played some part and that we may not be complete strangers to the concept of punitive accountability.

This, then, has been the reality for educational research for some time – caught in a continual re-enactment of Nelson holding his telescope to his blind eye and claiming to see no ships. Politicians north and south of the border make considerable play of research informing their policies, yet those policies are radically different and therefore the research they quote to back up these policies mirrors that difference.

And when it comes to finding research to back up a favoured policy, goodness knows they are spoiled for choice. Despite the lack of funding, we are neither short of research to quote, nor bereft of evidence to consider. The OECD seems to be offering me more grist to my mill every time I open my Twitter feed, and that's only one source. All of which leads us to consider a very important question: how do we decide what we believe?

I suggest there are three filters we can use, the first of which is our *values*. The worst tendency is to use research only for confirmation. Too often, its sole role is to substantiate a position or view that has already been adopted. Yet, for research to have any true transformative merit, there has to be a willingness to consider its implications fully. The key then is to reflect on one's own values as a result of these new insights. Research itself will never be value free so, fundamentally, the research debate should be informed by the debate on values. Values are formed by so many influences and go so deep that they must be one of the filters by which we judge the evidence and the research. However, if one has no values, no core principles, how can one have consistency or integrity in the light of new information? We need to have an ideology; the trick is not to become an ideologue. We must remain open to question and to the evolution of ideas while remaining true to our values.

Values alone are not enough when it comes to exploring educational research – *experience* needs to play a part too as we determine our view on new insights. Again this is double edged. Unwillingness to re-examine the lessons of experience is a pretty good working definition of complacency. However, if research flies in the face of the apparent lessons of our reality, it is perhaps more important to question the research. 'The facts are wrong' as Einstein is purported to have said. Such an approach has brought benefits. For example, many Scottish schools with which I've had contact adhered to the use of phonics when the favoured research suggested other approaches to the teaching of reading. As a result they maintained a balanced and blended approach to developing literacy, which benefitted their children.

The third filter, closely aligned to experience, is *common sense* – that sustaining cocktail of life lessons, principles and healthy questioning that can seem in all too short supply when politicians make their decrees, their telescope held up to their one bad eye. As an education professional we must always remember to ask ourselves one important question: in the light of all I know and who I am, and taking into account my ambitions for those I teach and serve, does this make sense to me?

Recommended book:

David Woods and Tim Brighouse, *The A–Z of School Improvement: Principles and Practice* (London: Bloomsbury Education, 2013)

Notes

1   T. Frank, *What's the Matter With America: The Resistible Rise of the American Right* (London: Vintage Books, 2011).

2   M. Fullan, keynote speech at the Edinburgh Learning Festival, 25 April 2014, summarised in G. Gilchrist, Michael Fullan in Edinburgh, *School Leadership – A Scottish Perspective* (26 April 2014). Available at: http://gg1952.blogspot.co.uk/2014_04_01_archive.html.

Chapter 19

Tell It Through Story
A Giant Curriculum

Trisha Lee

Watch any group of children engaged in fantasy play and you will see how effortlessly they incorporate narrative and metaphor into their lives. From a young age, children have the capacity to jump seamlessly between acting out characters and discussing complex plot developments. In make-believe play they solve problems, process ideas and use objects symbolically with ease and to great effect.

The collaborative nature of story play supports children's acquisition of emotional intelligence and helps develop their language and communication abilities. Through taking on different roles they examine the world from diverse viewpoints. They study the consequences of a character's actions and negotiate with others around challenging storylines. And the best thing of all, this happens instinctively – children are experts at this stuff.

Imagine if we could capture this drive to discover and incorporate it in all aspects of our classroom.

Let's look at it from an adult perspective. Whenever we receive new information we remember only a fraction of it in our normal lives. Once you've finished reading this book only a small percentage of it will stay with you. You will need to reread it again and again to tap into its full potential.

However, it is much easier to remember if we are given information in story form. The research – and my own experience – tells us this.[1] To prove my point, in the training I do with teachers I read out a list of items and ask questions on it. No one knows the answers because, even though they were keen, they did not remember what they had been told. Then I read out another list, which this time is in narrative form. Now when I ask questions they *all* know *all* the answers. Another example of the power of story is when I give them a series of disconnected sentences and get the delegates to connect them by creating a narrative. Not only do they always manage this, they also add a vast amount of detail that was not included in any of the original sentences.

So how can we incorporate stories into our classrooms, employing this tool to engage even those children who are often left behind?

By way of an example, let's explore some possibilities for a story based curriculum using the theme of giants. There are hundreds of giant stories and a Giant Curriculum, with a spice of imagination, can incorporate any of these for children from nursery to Year 7.

So, if you're sitting comfortably …

I want you to visualise a terrible storm, and to pretend that we, the villagers, are shut in our houses, too frightened to leave. Eventually the storm breaks and we emerge and travel around our neighbourhood, trying to assess the damage. It doesn't look good. Suddenly we come across an object, a giant object, and people start asking questions.

Now, what could the object be? Perhaps it's a giant footprint? Or a giant shoe? It could be a massive toothbrush, or maybe it's an enormous piece of clothing? Whatever it is, it forces us to construct a narrative to explain how it got there. Regardless of whether this is from the viewpoint of the villagers or from the perspective of the owner, immediately we have a story to tell.

Next we can 'explode' this topic into a mathematical enquiry. Using the object, we could try to discover how tall its owner might be. Remember that in story we need a reason for our investigation, so maybe we want to know its height in order to find out where it is hiding. After all, we still don't know if the giant is safe. We then find ourselves launched into an exploration of the golden mean, where the proportions of our body follow certain rules. For example, did you know that each of us is between six and seven of our own feet tall? That the span of your arms is approximately the same as the length of your body for many people (but not everyone)? That half your width, from the top of your finger to the tip of your nose, is about five lengths of your hand, and your foot fits neatly into the space between your elbow and your wrist?

Supposing your object is a giant toothbrush, what non-standard measurements can you use to work out the height of the giant? Do different approaches yield different results? Try sticking down masking tape lines to mark out the various responses. This is a great way of exploring maths, but maths that has no right or wrong answer.

The enquiry continues to grow as we investigate how to capture our giant. Just how do you go about catching a giant? If you dig a hole, how deep does it have to be? If you build a net, what dimensions should it have?

What's more, the story can twist. Supposing our giant is friendly, we must then work out what tasks are involved in looking after her. (Is it a her? How do we know?) This in itself is a highly mathematical endeavour, as anyone who has read *Gulliver's Travels* will tell you. How much food does a giant eat? How can we make a loaf of bread large enough for a giant jam sandwich? How much jam do we need to cover each slice? Suddenly we are involved in surface area, measuring and scaling up recipes, or taking mean, median and mode averages of the number of peas each of us have at a meal and then working out how many times more than that we will need to satisfy a giant appetite. What if our giant wants a party and invites four friends? We can use circumference to make giant plates, scale to create party hats or pattern to make a giant tablecloth.

But wait! What happens if our giant eats too much and becomes ill? Maybe we'll need to go inside her and find out what's wrong. Yuk! Suddenly we are in the realms of biomedical science and have the opportunity to act out the process of digestion, engaging the class in becoming a giant oesophagus, pushing and squeezing the food down to the stomach, before churning it up. Once inside the giant's body, children can share what they know about their internal organs and become researchers finding out about viruses and blood cells to make the giant better.

We can also examine the social and philosophical issues around living with giants. Is it right that we keep her in our town? Should we be allowed to climb on her? What does she need to make her happy? What would a giant society look like? What are their rules? For literacy, we can examine the many giant stories in literature and think about why we find them fascinating.

And so it goes, a Giant Curriculum slowly unfolding. Letting individual interests determine the stages of the enquiry would enable different groups to be engaged in separate activities. One could make giant clothes, another might investigate how high giants can jump, another could build a miniature town from a giant's perspective.

The possibilities are, like a child's imagination, gigantic.

Recommended book:

Kendall Haven, *Story Proof: The Science Behind the Startling Power of Story* (Westport, CT: Libraries Unlimited, 2007)

Notes

1   See L. Widrich, The Science of Storytelling: Why Telling a Story Is the Most Powerful Way To Activate Our Brains, *Life Hacker* (12 May 2012). Available at: http://lifehacker.com/5965703/the-science-of-storytelling-why-telling-a-story-is-the-most-powerful-way-to-activate-our-brains.

Chapter 20

Tiny Worlds

Dung Beetles, Cosmic Drama and the Educational Imperative

Professor Paul Clarke

Unless we live our lives with at least some cosmological awareness, we risk collapsing into tiny worlds. For we can be fooled into thinking that our lives are passed in political entities, such as a state or nation; or that the bottom-line concerns in life have to do with economic realities of consumer lifestyles. In truth, we live in the midst of immensities and we are intricately woven into a great cosmic drama.

Brian Swimme, *The Hidden Heart of the Cosmos* (1996)

Consider the dung beetle, *Scarabaeus sacer*.[1] Prior to embarking on a journey, it climbs onto its freshly created dung ball and dances around in circles on the top. Despite our desire for fancy, this is not a whimsical display of delight at their latest accumulation of fresh faeces. It is actually a sophisticated method of navigation, inspired by the fact that the dung beetle wants to establish the most direct escape route from rival beetles looking to steal their neatly crafted ball. Due to the dung ball being spherical, if they don't have a clear idea of where they are going they run the risk of literally rolling round in circles and ending up back in the dung where they started. However, their clever navigational alignment technique ensures that they are able to roll to their desired location in a direct line. And what do they align themselves to in order to navigate? Well, according to Marie Dacke of Lund University in Sweden, they use the Milky Way.[2]

I was ruminating on this coleopterologistic[3] fact recently with my friends, a motley crew consisting of an artist, a geologist, a theologian, an ecologist, a quantum physicist, a charity director, a teacher, a filmmaker and Sharpie, our local indigenous guide, sitting around a crackling fire one evening in the wilderness of South Australia's Flinders Ranges. We had gathered for a four day retreat to discuss educational purpose and practice against the magnificent backdrop of the Flinders wilderness. In particular we were vexed by the question: what is the purpose of education in a time of ecological change?

My argument was simple. Perhaps we should take seriously the cosmic drama of the alignment techniques of the humble dung beetle, and take note of its point of reference – the universal.

Attention to the universal, the cosmological,[4] to the very big picture, is not a dominant feature of daily educational practice or narrative in our schools. What schooling tends to orientate towards is a diet of pragmatic realism defined, in the main, by the limited imagination of our industrial mind and consumerist experience. What we educate young people for is to function as effective citizens inside the industrial growth economy, as if that world order is the way it always has been and the way it always will be. We train them, therefore, to think in particular ways, which in turn enable them to function socially and economically. Ivan Illich describes this as our collective 'schooled mind'.[5] The given definition and practice of education is, as a result, embedded within a construct of human proportions, nothing bigger. It takes very seriously human interest and human predilections, but not much more. It is temporal, of the moment, of our existing interests and interpretations. This would probably be acceptable if it maintained a degree of awareness of the cosmological, but it doesn't.

And that's a dangerous state of affairs.

Despite all the PhDs, MBAs, diplomas and certificates, the crises arising from modern schooling and educational provision are evident all around us. For example, we continue to witness human activity that relentlessly degrades and destroys the planet's natural life systems. It seems our great intelligence fails us when we have to imagine beyond our individual and collective human sized spheres. Perhaps, instead, what we need, in addition to tapping into the brilliance of the human mind, is a sensitivity and recognition of the potential of the scale of the universal. In the huge developments in science and technology, we have established a degree of control over some natural processes, but in so doing we have not come to understand the sheer magnitude of what we are a part of. Rather than using science to connect us with nature, we have fallen into a trap of convincing ourselves of our autonomy, of our separateness from nature.

This illusory sense of control grows exponentially, and those of us in the developed world begin to believe ever more fervently that we can resolve, somehow, any problem we encounter. We have come to believe in the illusion of certainty and of our own superiority in a view of realty that is entirely anthropomorphic. This is a problematic belief. It leads us to assume that we can transcend natural limits. It leads us to deny the reality of our dependence on the natural world. And we are starting to observe the consequences of this fantasy all around us.

This hubris applies to societies as much as it does to individuals. It is woven into the fabric of our political and economic systems. The prevailing economic model of industrial growth is predicated on the notion of a world without limits. This has led to an over-exploitation of nature's resources and is in the process of overwhelming the biosphere. The result is the planetary crisis we now face, where climate change, mass species extinction, habitat degradation and environmental collapse are not a possibility or even a probability but an inevitability.[6] It is a scenario with potentially devastating consequences for all living beings.

What saddens me as someone who has worked in schools and across the school system for many years is that this is, and always has been, entirely predictable. It is a direct result of how we educate and the manner in which we school the individual and collective mind. It is therefore *a problem of, and a problem for,* schools. It is *the* educational question for our time.

At the point where we begin to recognise the magnitude of the ecological challenge before us, we also begin to identify other narratives that can illuminate alternative notions of progress.

We are recognising that opposites can both attract and inform. For example, quantum science, cosmology and spirituality can all help us to establish an understanding of our human presence on earth as one that is in consort with other earth life. As this knowledge grows, we simultaneously begin to recognise the reality of nature as a truly universal, cosmological entity, which creative arts can further illuminate to facilitate insight and cultural understanding. Through this understanding we can reimagine the human experience as one which entertains a multiplicity of relationships – to self, to other beings, to places, to frames of time – and which could provide a way forward for us.

We are recognising too that the outer physical environment has a direct impact on our inner emotional one. As Thomas Berry says, 'We see that what happens to non-human also happens to human. We see that if the outer world is degraded, then the inner world too, is diminished.'[7] An impoverished physical environment degrades everything, from the spiritual, emotional, imaginative and creative through to the intellectual and sensual. Likewise, an impoverished schooling, limited to the imaginative frame of the ego, is not going to bear witness to the radical adjustments required by our species as we confront the magnitude of global natural systems change in the coming decades.

Our cosmological encounter with the dung beetle is therefore a symbol of a transcendent opportunity. It imagines a different form of the tiny world we inhabit, one which deals with the immediate need of time and place, but is also recognisably connected to immensities. I see this as a prompt, asking us to consider what we use as our own compass to provide orientation as educators, both for ourselves and with others. It provokes us to establish our point of reference as something that steps away from the purely human centric and realigns us with the cosmological.

It is time to break the existing frame. In so doing we get to redefine our concept of personal and collective purpose and priority, realigning it with a better understanding of life as a whole, all life. At this point, the educational imperative changes from the utilitarian and anthropocentric to one that embraces sustainable forms of progress. We will have shifted our frame of schooling from the ego to the eco, with progress measured by the growth of our cosmological mind.

I have already hinted that I think we have to start by considering the cognitive map, and re-framing this to attend to the ecological as a core component of our interpretive frame. Forget national centric curricula, forget child centred learning, these are simply versions of the same ego – human centric and forged through industrialisation. The imperative of education has to become the ecological. How to educate the ecological mind as the basis of the human psyche is our way forward.

In developing an ecological mind we start to form the conditions for universal alignment, the sustainable conditions for life.[8] These are practical actions focused on our own presence within a renewable earth system, one which is framed within a cosmological pattern and which navigates towards a more sustainable future.

So where to begin? It doesn't matter, but begin outside and connect with the environment immediately present. It may be entirely urban; again, it doesn't matter. This is just the beginning. We can do it in simple stages but we always attend to the small and the universal; that is, the pattern. We might begin in the schoolyard, on the roof, under a tree, we might even begin in the intestines, the microbial, the tiny worlds which in turn expose the immensities around us. Lie in the gut and look at the stars.

Whatever we select, we focus on the universal principle that everything is connected to every-thing else, now and forever. What is this place we are living in? How does this system func-tion to sustain life? Where are the crisis points? Where is the evidence of possibility? Where might we grow something, nurturing life? Where might we observe cloud formation, water movement, traffic pollution? What did we eat today? Where is it from? What is it made of? Once the alignment occurs the cognitive frame opens out and the universal pattern, the way everything is connected to everything else, becomes obvious. Even a child can see it. Even a dung beetle can see it.

My interest in working in partnership across a global school network lies in the exploration and exposition of this great work to begin a narrative that conceives social change as an interconnected community moving towards a sustainable and resilient presence. If we reconcile these tensions and make progress, it will be through the cultural, economic, social and political transformation of schooling, realigning it as one that moves us towards a sustainable civilisation.

The project that my colleagues and I are undertaking is to design, develop and sustain an enquiry into the paradox that exists between existing school spaces and places and how to move them to the next evolutionary state of practice, and to do this by reimagining these spaces and places through an ecological lens. To do this we have begun to create Earthcare Centres. These are both real and virtual – they can be at a school or in a derelict warehouse, on a laptop computer or in a jungle or a desert space. We are exploring these ideas by connecting people, place and nature, and how we do this is a part of the experimental project framework. It is undefined, open ended and emergent. It looks like good learning should look like. We are intent on developing an arena within which critical investigation, exposition and illustration can play out to elicit deeper levels of understanding and interpretation of the human condition and its place within a wider natural system. It is this relationship which forms our investigative question: how can we live as *a part of, not apart from*, nature?

This is the purpose of education in an ecological age. It begins, I think, to define the next iteration of what we currently call 'school'.

Recommended book:

David Abram, *The Spell of the Sensuous: Perception and Language in a More-Than-Human World* (New York: Vintage, 1997)

Notes

1 This is the scarab beetle as worshipped by the ancient Egyptians.

2 M. Dacke, E. Baird, M. Byrne, C. H. Scholtz and E. J. Warrant, Dung Beetles Use the Milky Way For Orientation, *Current Biology* 23(4) (2013): 298–300.

3 Yes, it's a word.

4 Cosmology, despite being hijacked by the hippies, is a serious study of the origins, structure and fate of the universe.

5 I. Illich, *Deschooling Society* (Open Forum) (London: Marion Boyars Publishers, 1995).

6 E. Kolbert, *The Sixth Extinction: An Unnatural History* (London: Bloomsbury, 2014).

7 T. Berry, *The Great Work: Our Way Into the Future* (London: Broadway, 2000), p. 200.

8 P. Clarke, The Cosmos of Connection: Re-Imagining Education For Ecological Consciousness (Catholic Education South Australia (CESA), 2015). Invitational paper drafted in response to Carla Rinaldi's *Reimagining Childhood: The Inspiration of Reggio Emilia Education Principles In South Australia* (Adelaide: Government of South Australia, 2013).

Chapter 21

There Isn't a Plaster For That!

Emotional Health Is a Whole School Issue, So What Can You Do?

Nina Jackson

What would you do …?
If a pupil told you on a Friday afternoon that they don't want to be in this world any more?

What would you do …?
If a pupil slit their wrist under a classroom desk with a blade from a pencil sharpener?

What would you do …?
If a pupil took an overdose in school, attended your lesson and later collapsed, and you knew nothing about it until another pupil tells you that they were seen crying in the toilet with a bottle of pills?

What would you do …?
If you saw bruises, burn marks and cuts on a pupil's ankle during the exam season?

What would you do …?
If a colleague 'didn't quite look right' in staff briefing and you just know something is wrong?

What would you do …?

If a teacher in your child's school had been off work for a few months and you'd heard it was severe depression and anxiety and they have now returned to work?

What would you do …?

If you felt emotionally unwell and you didn't know why? You don't want to get out of bed and everything is, well, just too much – and it's been going on for a few months and you've been telling yourself it will all be OK, but it isn't?

The truth is, most teachers don't know what to do about these 'real life' situations (yes, each one is true). They don't really feel equipped to deal with emotional and mental health issues. They want to help but, well, there isn't a plaster in the first aid kit for any of them.

One in four of us will experience mental illness or emotional difficulties during our lifetime – the spectrum of experiences is huge. It could be someone in your school, a family member or you. Would you feel ashamed of feeling that way, whatever 'that way' is? Would you feel ashamed if it was a member of your class? Your staff? Your family?

Mental and emotional health issues are on the increase, and we are seeing more and more pupils and staff having to deal with these problems in schools. However, there is a severe lack of understanding, and a dark cloud hangs over even the mention of mental illness, with many people embarrassed to talk about it or seek help due to the stigma attached to it. There is even a taboo about talking to, or about, 'crazy people' because they are dangerous too! And the media doesn't help.

All I can do in this short chapter is to raise awareness of the issue, but that itself can help to break through the stigma. It might instigate a conversation, which is a big start. So, try to see this as just the beginning of what we should, could and need to do for education and for humanity. There is no need to be embarrassed about mental and emotional health issues (although many of us still are).

There is no formal element in initial teacher education and training courses that covers mental and emotional health issues, but there should be. After all, we are dealing with human emotions every day. If it's a daily part of our various 'learning journeys' then we should also have some understanding and insight into what we could do when we are confronted with students with emotional problems. Ultimately, it's about being able to support each other and the children we teach.

There are so many areas within mental and emotional health care. It's like a giant library of technical and medical terms. Every shelf is full of books on different conditions and levels of depression and anxiety (the two most commonly diagnosed forms of mental illness), self-harm, grief, stress, bipolar disorder, panic attacks, schizophrenia, delirium, delusions, hallucinations and many more. Did you know, for example, that attention deficit hyperactive disorder (ADHD) is a diagnosed mental health disorder? What's more, in some rare cases children can 'grow out of it'?[1] It's a tricky concept to grasp.

When a person is experiencing mental and emotional health issues they often can't articulate what's wrong or how they are feeling – they just know that things aren't right. There will be some who choose to call for help in the most traumatic of ways (traumatic for you, but 'right' for them), such as self-harming and then disclosing this by revealing scars or cuts, or just casually making sure you can see them. Some may attempt suicide by taking an overdose, trying to hang themselves or other methods. Difficult as this may be for you to comprehend, this might be the only way they know how to cry out for help at that time. And there are those whose cries are less dramatic, such as the individuals who just withdraw. Remember, each 'cry' or 'call' might be different for each individual but they all still count.

As a starting point in considering what you could do if faced with a pupil or colleague with what you believe may be a mental and emotional health issue, I have some suggestions for you. I've made these simple and compassionate rather than too complex. In this way, you can at least make a start in being there for them – although when you need to seek proper medical help, make sure you do.

- **Ask.** If you sense that something isn't quite right, stop and ask the person if everything is alright, even if you don't know them that well. When you ask, 'How are *you*?' (with the emphasis on that last word), you will be amazed how people respond. Even if they are fine, at least they will know you care.

- **Listen.** Take time to listen. If someone is in need and they know what they are feeling may be different or 'not right' for them, just listen to what they have to say. Don't judge them or try to give immediate answers, but aim to make them feel safe. Concentrate on what they are saying, even if you can't make sense of it at that time. Listening with your head slightly to one side can make you seem like a more sympathetic physical and psychological listener.

- **Talk.** Talking is one of the most powerful tools we have as human beings. Talking things through, however complex the issue may feel at that time, can save another person from the depths of despair. You may not be able to understand their feelings or perspective, but just communicating with someone who is going through a difficult time can be life-saving. Literally.

- **Reassurance.** Reassure the person that with help and support they can get through the emotional trauma they are experiencing. Comfort them with the thought that, together and with help, they can find a way of making things better. Reassurance is all about starting points; only then is it about knowing who to get involved. Depending on the severity of the call for help it may be a parent, doctor, friend or a colleague – each situation will have its own path. However, start by assuring the person that they are safe. And, yes, I keep repeating the word 'safe', because that is what a person experiencing mental and emotional distress needs as the first step towards recovery.

• **Time for you.** When you have been involved in supporting a person with mental and emotional health problems, it's extremely important that you also make time for *you*. The physical, psychological and emotional strength you may have used in supporting others can be a mind-zapping experience for you too. Many of us forget that. It's about getting the balance right and knowing that you cannot be there for others unless you look after yourself. And I mean that, otherwise you will end up feeling 'not quite right' yourself.

In this brief chapter, I've attempted to take a very realistic and humanistic approach to a massive topic, which teachers often feel we don't have the skills or training to cope with. That said, if a child fell off their bike and had hurt themselves and were crying, with even the smallest of cuts, would you go to their rescue? Of course you would.

Why is it, then, that because there isn't a physical plaster or an obvious sign that someone is hurt inside, and experiencing the most dreadful emotional trauma, that we wouldn't go out of our way to help them? It's because most people are scared of mental illness and worry about what is the right thing to do. It's a taboo area where things might get awkward and difficult. But it doesn't have to be that way. Not any more.

I have only scratched the surface here by posing some questions and attempting to give you some advice using the simplest of approaches. But let's not forget that mental and emotional health issues are complex and different for each person. They take time to unravel. They need care. They require a non-judgemental mindset, which many people struggle with, especially if such issues are outside of their own experience. But if that is the case – if you are one of the three in four people to escape mental health problems – then count yourself lucky.

The current educational climate of high pressure, high stakes testing with punitive, top down control mechanisms is making for an environment that is ripe for mental and well-being problems in young people, their teachers and their school leaders. So it is important for you to know what to do if someone turned to you tomorrow for help. Reaching for a plaster is pointless, so what would you do?

Recommended book:

Kay Redfield Jamison, *An Unquiet Mind: A Memoir of Moods and Madness* (London: Picador, 2011)

Notes

1 See http://www.action.org.uk/our-research/attention-deficit-hyperactivity-disorder-adhd-why-do-some-children-grow-out-their-disor.

Chapter 22

From Attention To Obsession

The Stuff, Strategies and Soul of Teaching and Learning

Hywel Roberts

Children dwell in the moment and bring immortality to that experience ... some days stay golden forever.

Professor Leonard George Marsh

When I started teaching, the main tension in the classroom was whether my classes would be interested enough in my lesson plan to behave appropriately. There were occasions when I even tried to make them feel bad for not doing as I'd asked with a bit of teacher guilt-trip-for-learning stuff. Biddable kids are like that. They won't go straight for the chair-chucking but, rather, sit there in a passive daze, occasionally offering a supportive but non-committal nod as you try to open up the world of the curriculum to them.

In these halcyon days, my pen and ink planning, coupled with the innovation of a marker pen whiteboard and hand drawn worksheets, were the tools of my well-intentioned but ultimately futile attempts at engagement. The mist lifted when I realised that I needed to plan for the *children in front of me*, not invest hours coming up with the greatest lesson ever created on Shakespeare's *Julius Caesar*. What I should have been doing was designing a lesson that would deepen their understanding of the Bard's Roman epic, whilst supporting the class in their understanding of what is a challenging text to a class of 14-year-olds from Barnsley.

The contemporary equivalent of this teacher's ability to hobble yourself before the lesson has even started now comes in two forms:

1. The downloading of 'brilliant' ready-made lesson plans from websites that actually fail in your hands because they were written for a particular class at a particular prep school in Kent. You, on the other hand, recently woke up in your flat in Cleethorpes. The abilities of the two classes may be very similar, but there are other important differences. And you, in doing the downloading and ignoring the need for filtering and making the material appropriate for your particular setting, have turned the act of teaching into a skill-less, soul-less act that could be done by a monkey after a few weeks of training.

2. The plugging in of that pen-drive/memory stick loaded with pre-written schemes of work. Basically, endless slides created by people you probably don't know for children they will never meet and handed lovingly to you by your lead teacher or head of department with a knowing look. Think of them as some sort of USB-Hoover with which your humanity, charisma, humour and all the other hard won attributes that make you a great teacher are sucked out of you, and you are left standing in front of a class, reading someone else's PowerPoint and wondering where it all went wrong.

The antidote to both these examples of inane teaching is the following heartfelt plea – *plan for your children in your classroom in your school in your community.*

If there is one saving grace, I suppose it is that they can offer some sort of inspiration to get you started. It's fine to look at the prep school planning and think, 'I could do something like that, but I will need to change some of it.' That's putting it through your filter. Just make sure you're not saying that in order to try to get yourself off the hook. Plan with your integrity and moral drive intact by remembering that you know your children best (or you should do). Rather than just reeling off the familiar off-the-shelf lesson plan when things are tense, combat dead time appropriately when you see it and don't be frightened of a bit of honest reflection.

Now there's a word: *reflection*. Throughout my career I've been instructed, like you, to reflect on how things have gone in a lesson or in a day. It's only in the last few years that I believe I've got any good at doing it. During teacher training we are asked to reflect in abundance, but we are often not given the tools to do so — some useful questions, maybe, or a pro forma reflection tool.

These days I find it helps to focus a lot of my reflection on how engaged the children I've been working with have been. It's the same when I'm working with adults. I spend a lot of energy on it. Engagement can be fuelled by great planning followed by genuine reflection. Or, in a nutshell, did I plan a lesson worth behaving for? It's amazing how uppity some people get when I suggest all teachers should pose this question. To me, these elements are vital to great learning, but it doesn't end there. There's also all the *other stuff*.

The stuff of setting the scene for learning:

+   Display. Ask the timeless reflection question: how does the space you work in reflect your attitude to learning, to the children and to yourself as a teacher?

+   Rapport. This is where as grown-ups we take on the role of kid-whisperers. It's a skill most teachers have and mere mortals who don't teach can't fathom.

+   Relationships. What do the children think you think of them? What is their evidence? Check out these genuine case studies. (Hey, I'm simply reporting back!)

Case study A

Me: *What do you think the teachers are thinking when they see you?*
Aruna (aged 14): *They're thinking, 'Oh no. It's them.'*
Me: Oh. *Er …*

Aruna (hitting her stride): *She doesn't even see us. She's too busy wanting to smash up her own computer.*[1] *Got her back to us. Not bothered.*

Me (pulling a Martin Freeman-bemused-hobbit-lost-for-words face): *Hmmmm …*

Case study B

Me: *What do you think the teachers are thinking when they see you?*
Oscar (aged 6): *Nothing. She loves us.*
Me: *Oh! Wow!*
Oscar: *If I had another teacher, I'd punch her in the face and go and find her.*
Me (doing another Freeman): *Ooooof …*

+ Classroom arrangement (rows, U-shapes, clusters, tribes, school canteen, different space, deep space, outside, the woods, the deep dark forest, the plague city, Mars).

+ Consistency. Consistency x 100. Break consistency down to its constituent parts and you'll see that it's everything you'd expect it to be – consistency of expectation, consequence, fairness, hope, enthusiasm, energy, challenge, seriousness, fun, kindness, professionalism, warm humour, reflection, botheredness.

The only thing that shouldn't be consistent is our repertoire of strategies that get us through the day. That's something that should be growing and developing all the time, like an augmented reality bookcase expanding in front of your very eyes and available 24/7 for you to reach out and grab, in the moment, with children you're working with. Your repertoire is your developing teacher expertise. It's there and fairly empty when you're a trainee but bulging at the seams by the time you're writing your retirement speech.

All this repertoire, all this stuff, is there to support you in engaging your learners. Some of it is straightforward common sense. Some of it is hard fought. Some of it is what you have discovered for yourself, often from your worst lessons. Some of it you have learned from master practitioners. I have worked with great teachers and learned from them all. One of the greatest was Dorothy Heathcote (run to Google now if you need to). She summed up everything I've been trying to say here in her continuum of engagement, which is a simple straight line. I've bent it around and turned it into a circle.

Adapted from Heathcote's continuum of engagement. Available at: http://www.mantleoftheexpert.com/resources/planning_resources/continuum%20of%20engagement.pdf.

This is the key reflection tool I turn to after I've done my best to take care of everything else. Like a lot of useful models it doesn't give us answers; rather it offers a framework on which to hang our thinking. When working in social, emotional and behavioural difficulties settings, for example, we work really hard to capture the children's *attention* and, through the use of appropriate strategies and the stuff I've talked about above, we gather *interest*. Sometimes that's as much as we can hope for in any setting. *Engagement* is the act of doing – the teacher's instruction and direction manifested as a human act, the doing by the children. And it doesn't have to be fun.

(A brief word on the concept of fun: I'm engaged in the activity of staying alive when I'm driving on the M25 but I'm not having any fun. When I was an apprentice gravedigger (I know!), I was engaged in digging graves and having completely no fun whatsoever. On occasion I'd be bricking it, which does not feature on the continuum. Fun, however, can be a happy and desirable outcome of engagement, can't it?)

The last two elements on the continuum are *investment* and *obsession*. Investment is where the children know *why* they are doing the activity and obsession is where they don't want it to end. Simple as that. They are *in* the learning. They see the benefits of it. They sometimes just don't want it to end:

Can I stay in at break?

I'm going to build my own castle this weekend!

I'm gonna bake for my mum this weekend.

Can we stay with you, Sir?

Recognise that sort of comment? I hope you do.

So Heathcote's model is the one I'm carrying around in my head to quality control the work I'm doing with children. As in any teacher's head, it's fighting for space with everything else we have to concern ourselves with day to day. But without it, I may well just be surviving. Just getting by. A reflective model such as this maintains and feeds our integrity as teachers. It fuels our desire to do the right thing. It stops the shrill voices on Twitter, or in the blogs, or in the not-that-impartial media from steering us away from what we know is right. It keeps you bothered to do the best for the kids and to help them get the best from themselves and from each other. It helps keep things proper golden.

Recommended book:

Cecily O'Neill (ed.), *Dorothy Heathcote on Education and Drama: Essential Writings* (Abingdon: Routledge, 2014)

Notes

1   The teacher is stressed out I reckon and has arrived moments before the children. Aruna has no sympathy though. She's 14.

Chapter 23

Is the Education System In This Country F#%ked?

Education, Inequality and Economic Fodder

Tait Coles

In 2012, a complex systems researcher with pink punk hair presented a paper to the American Geophysical Union. It was entitled 'Is Earth F#%ked?' and made Brad Werner a hero in environmental circles for telling it how it is. If I were to be asked the same question, but about the education system in this country, I would have to say quite simply, 'Yes. Very.'

As with Brad Werner, sometimes such language is the only thing that not only describes the situation succinctly but also serves to wake people up at the same time. It gets across the fact that the education system in this country – the one I work in, day in, day out – is broken, corrupt and rotten. Please note too that I deliberately use the word 'system' for that is what it is, one that has been carefully constructed and controlled for decades by the hegemony to serve the interests of the few.

Education in this country is a sorting mechanism that classifies young people based on their class, wealth, race and ethnicity, all in the false guise of improving the lives of future generations.[1] As Paulo Freire's beautifully direct quote implies, 'The education that the dominant classes offer to the working class is the education that reproduces the working class.'[2]

We have a system that is designed for and rewards only white middle-class students.[3] Those who look, think, talk and act like those in power will ultimately succeed and excel. Meanwhile, the majority of students who suffer in our educational apartheid are from different backgrounds and communities than those who are controlling this unjust system. As Pierre Bourdieu suggests, education produces a 'cultural reproduction', whereby schools only recognise and reward middle-class knowledge, language and culture.[4]

Don't be fooled: government (of every political persuasion) claims of driving up standards, providing extra funding for students from families with low incomes and 'doing the best for our disadvantaged' pupils are all propaganda. Young people's futures are being used as a currency for their political gains. We have schools acting as an 'ideological state apparatus', indoctrinating students into believing that the status quo of society and their education is both fair and legitimate.[5]

But what about the individual 'success stories' of black and minority ethnic students or schools with above average numbers of free school meals students which outperform their affluent school counterparts? This is explained by the Faustian bargain that educators have taken to de-culturalise their pupils and convince them into believing that it is necessary to cast off their own backgrounds, values and culture in order for them to become 'successful' and 'achieve'.[6]

The only way our 'disadvantaged' students can win in this system is to leave behind their beliefs and communities in order to assimilate the societal 'norms' of the white middle classes. We should never ask young people in a so-called democratic and multicultural society to make a choice between hardship and changing who they are in order to succeed and conform.

So why are we hoodwinked by this scandal? Media and governments (the lapdogs of the corporate neoliberal giants) work tirelessly to disguise the fact that inequality exists in our society, and they work even harder to conceal that this disparity is perpetuated by our education system. As Henry A. Giroux recently observed, our understanding of the world through the media we consume ensures that 'political illiteracy and moral tranquilisation work in tandem to produce the authoritarian subject, willing to participate in their own oppression.'[7]

Shockingly, the disguised partisan methodology of inequality *through* education is abundant in almost every school you set foot in. Schools are unconsciously, and in some heinous cases deliberately, becoming the vehicles for social reproduction, churning out repressed subjects to fill their predetermined places in our unjust and unfair society.

The current popular wave of identikit teaching manuals (most notably Doug Lemov's *Teach Like a Champion*; the 'discerning' choice of Teach First[8]) which advocate classroom practices based on oppressive disciplinary rules and celebrate authoritarian pedagogy is a right-wing attempt to subordinate schools, deskill teachers and oppress its students in order to fulfil the needs of the capital. This is not education; this is domestication. There was a time when ideology prevailed in the classroom; now it appears – through Lemovian practice – that only *white* privilege fills the classroom.

It must be pointed out that the 'progressive' arm of teaching – those who vehemently argue against these conservative and traditional methods of teaching – may, in fact, through their own classroom routines, expectations and strategies, also be unconsciously preparing students to develop the traits of the obedient and meek; the perfect attributes of the submissive and oppressed.

We are grooming kids to become economic fodder for the corporate powers that ultimately shape and determine what should be taught and how. The end result? To maintain and legitimise a class-divided society of those who have and those who have not.

There is no argument to this injustice; there is only apathy.

I am only too aware of the pressure on classroom teachers and school leaders to ensure that every student leaves school with the adequate number and quality of qualifications as determined (and altered on a regular basis) by governments. However, I struggle conscientiously and veraciously to ensure that all my students are educated both to achieve the grades that give them the potential to improve their life chances but also allow them to gain a comprehensive realisation and understanding of *their* world and a desire to improve it – and where necessary, change it. Our students need to learn the capacity of love before they have the courage to fight for it.

There has never before been so great a need for emancipatory education in this country. Emancipation is the act of liberation and freedom from controlling powers and conventions. True emancipation, however, is a self-regulated process where the individual achieves emancipation rather than it being done to them. The narcissistic notion of making a difference to a child by educating them so that they can 'escape' from their lives and background is frankly a disgusting and immoral one. Classroom teachers and school leaders need to consider Gert Biesta's idea of 'demystifying' what is hidden from the everyday views of those being oppressed, rather than indoctrinating students into a mould that society and schools have already defined for them.[9]

In a stagnant educational landscape, which currently seems unshakable and rebukes anyone who attempts to disrupt or subvert it, we need voices of dangerous and courageous thinking.[10] I believe that as educators we have a moral obligation not simply to comment on how wrong our education system is, but to use the power and opportunity we all have to change it. A reluctance to fight against it, and acts of neutrality and passivity, mean that every day you play your part in this nefarious sorting mechanism that we call education.

Recommended book:

Paulo Freire, *Pedagogy of the Oppressed*, tr. M. B. Ramos (London: Penguin, 1996)

Notes

1   The 2009 Nuffield Review concluded that the education system for 14–19-year-olds was tailored to serve the interests of richer students. See *Education For All: The Future of Education and Training For 14–19 Year Olds: Summary, Implications and Recommendations* (2009). Available at: http://www.nuffieldfoundation.org/sites/default/files/files/Nuffield%20Report28-04-09%20final%20to%20print.pdf. The inequality of our education system is also described in a 2014 Sutton Trust report, *Open Access: An Independent Evaluation*. The findings show that between the ages of 26 and 42 someone who attends an independent school will earn a total of £193,700 more than someone who attends a state school. Even when factors such as family background and early educational achievement are taken into account, the wage difference between state and independent schooling is a staggering £57,653. See Sutton Trust, Private School Premium of £194,000 Revealed In New Report [press release] (3 July 2014). Available at: http://www.suttontrust.com/newsarchive/private-school-premium-194000-revealed-new-report/.

David Gillborn analysed official Department for Education statistics and found that if these trends continue then the black and white inequality of student achievement will be permanent. Based on a 10-year trend, 'The soonest that Black students would hit 100 per cent, and finally close the gap, is 2054.' He adds, 'the present incremental changes in attainment, accompanied by self-congratulatory "Gap Talk", disguise a situation where pronounced racial inequalities of attainment are effectively locked-in as a permanent feature of the system'. See D. Gillborn, *Racism and Education: Coincidence or Conspiracy?* (Abingdon: Routledge, 2008), p. 68.

And, if this wasn't enough, it appears that no matter how academically successful you are, your religion may hold you back. Using data from the Office for National Statistics' Labour Force Survey of more than half a million people, Dr Nabil Khattab and Professor Ron Johnston found that Muslims were the most disadvantaged in terms of employment prospects out of 14 ethno-religious groupings in the UK. Muslim men were up to 76% less likely to have a job of any kind compared to white, male British Christians of the same age and with the same qualifications. And Muslim women were up to 65% less likely to be employed than their white Christian counterparts. See R. Dobson, British Muslims Face Worst Job Discrimination of Any Minority Group, According To Research, *The Independent* (30 November 2014). Available at: http://www.independent.co.uk/news/uk/home-news/british-muslims-face-worst-job-discrimination-of-any-minority-group-9893211.html.

2   M. Horton and P. Freire, *We Make the Road By Walking: Conversations On Education and Social Change* (Philadelphia, PA: Temple University Press, 1990), p. 213.

3   Research from the LSE suggests that young people from lower social class backgrounds and

ethnic minority groups are less likely to be offered a university place even with sufficient academic attainment. See London School of Economics and Political Science, Black and Ethnic Minority Students Less Likely To Receive Offers From University Than White Students [press release] (23 July 2014). Available at: http://www.lse.ac.uk/newsAndMedia/news/archives/2014/07/ BMEStudentsLessLikelyToReceiveOffersFromUniversity.aspx. As Dave Hill asked: 'Are the schools' formal curriculum and the hidden curriculum deliberately geared to failing most working class children, and to elevating, middle-and upper-class children above them?' See D. Hill, Social Class and Education, in D. Matheson and I. Grosvenor (eds), *An Introduction To the Study of Education* (London: David Fulton, 1999), pp. 84–102 at p. 93.

This supports Basil Bernstein's theory of class specific language (see B. Bernstein, *Class, Codes and Control: Theoretical Studies Towards a Sociology of Language* (London: Routledge & Kegan Paul, 1971)), where schools only reward middle-class 'elaborated code' and devalue working-class 'restricted code'. The commonly seen and heard mantra of 'Standard English' means that schools now promote monolingual 'mainstream' power codes as the only form of oracy used in classrooms, denying and oppressing students' own codes of communication. As David E. Kirkland observes, there is a need for schools to promote the 'linguistic pluralism' of their students, 'fully appreciating the hybrid and textured nature in which English is practiced and performed' by working-class and black and minority ethnic students, through legacies of survival and oppression. We need to respect that this is essential for successful literacy education. See D. E. Kirkland, English(es) in Urban Contexts: Politics, Pluralism, and Possibilities, *English Education* 42(3) (2010): 293–306 at 293. Available at: http://steinhardt.nyu.edu/scmsAdmin/uploads/006/176/English%28es%29%20in%20Urban%20 Contexts.pdf.

4   It is also important to think about what is meant by the terms 'high culture' and how it is accepted and promoted in schools, as compared to the disparaging educational view of the 'low and popular culture' of the working classes. See P. Bourdieu, *Distinction: A Social Critique of the Judgement of Taste* (Abingdon: Routledge, 2010 [1984]).

At this point it is relevant to mention E. D. Hirsch's idea of promoting a 'common core' in US schools, now being reproduced in many UK academies and free schools. Hirsch argues for a curriculum based on a common core in which he (and two other white, middle-class, male university professors) identified 5,000 items that every American student had to know to be 'culturally literate'. He suggests that cultural literacy, 'enables them to take up a newspaper and read it with an adequate level of comprehension' – further indication of conservative education and corporate-controlled media symbiotically working to produce passive consumers. Hirsch suggests that only by 'freezing a culture' can essential content become standardised. See E. D. Hirsch, *Cultural Literacy: What Every American Needs To Know* (New York: Random House, 1988), p. xiii.

In a paper endorsed by the National Council of Professors of Educational Administration (NCPEA), Fenwick English analyses Hirsch's work. He finds that 'On his list of 575 famous persons, 247 were Americans and of those 75% were white males. Clearly, when culture is frozen so are the dominant and privileged social structures which define "literacy". With echoes of Bourdieu, the paper argues that 'Schools serve as the legitimizers of a form of cultural capital and preserve and retain the culture of the elites who are at the helm of social power.' See F. English, The Ten Most Wanted Enemies of American Public Education's School Leadership, *International Journal of Educational Leadership Preparation* 5(3) (2010): 1–9. Available at: http://cnx.org/contents/a3319c24-23ee-4e25-bef5-75b13a5f542c@4.

5   In his essay on the ideological state apparatus (ISA), Louis Althusser examines the ways in which the state exerts control over its subjects in order to reproduce its productive power. He suggests that the educational apparatus – or school – is the dominant ideological state apparatus in capitalist formations for securing the reigning ideology. See L. Althusser, Ideology and Ideological State Apparatuses (1971), in *Lenin and Philosophy and Other Essays*, tr. B. Brewster (London: Monthly Review Press, 2001), pp. 121–176.

6   Many are displaying a perfect example of Derrick Bell's 'interest convergence', where racial advances and successes are only encouraged and supported when they promote white self-interest.

7   H. A. Giroux, Killing Machines and the Madness of Militarism: From Gaza To Afghanistan, *Truthout* (24 July 2014). Available at: http://www.truth-out.org/opinion/item/25136-killing-machines-and-the-madness-of-militarism-from-gaza-to-afghanistan.

8   D. Lemov, *Teach Like a Champion: 49 Techniques That Put Students On the Path To College* (San Francisco, CA: Jossey-Bass, 2010). Available in all 'good and outstanding' schools!

9   In *The Beautiful Risk of Education* (Boulder, CO: Paradigm, 2013), Gert Biesta writes about emancipation being ultimately contingent upon the truth; the truth uncontaminated by power. Earlier, writing in *Jacques Rancière: Education, Truth, Emancipation* (London: Continuum, 2010), Charles Bingham and Gert Biesta suggest that 'truth [that] can only be generated by someone who is positioned outside the influence of ideology' (p. 30). In order for students to achieve emancipation, someone else, who is not subjected to the workings of power, needs to provide them with an account of their conditions. In essence, 'the truth' can only be communicated by someone who is not being influenced; by someone who is not subjected to the power that needs to be overcome. The act of 'demystification' falls to the critical educator who must 'make visible what is hidden for those who are

the "object" of the emancipatory endeavors of the critical educator … making visible what is hidden from the everyday view' (p. 26). Educators need to check their own privilege in order to gain an adequate insight into the power relations in their teaching and learning situations, which is Immanuel Kant's pedagogical paradox: 'How do I cultivate freedom through coercion?'

10 See H. A. Giroux, Thinking Dangerously In An Age of Political Betrayal, *Truthout* (14 July 2014). Available at: http://truth-out.org/opinion/item/24869-henry-a-giroux-thinking-dangerously-in-an-age-of-political-betrayal.

Chapter 24

If You Change the Way You Look At Things, the Things You Look At Will Change

Taking a Restorative Approach Across School Communities

Mark Finnis

I remember it well, and I'm still not sure whether I should have laughed, cried or been really angry. Maybe all three.

I was sitting in a school reception reading a list of values the school had expensively printed and proudly displayed on the wall for all to see. 'Respect' was on the list, of course. I was reading it while, at the same time, a teacher was shouting loudly, aggressively and relentlessly directly into the face of a student. Like I say, what do you do – laugh, cry or fume? What would you do?

I don't relate this story to highlight bad teaching or the hypocrisy that schools – and other organisations, to be fair – demonstrate on a daily basis. I share it with you because I know, through years of work, that there is another way.

Restorative practice, with its emphasis on relationships, is not simply a trendy new strategy to put on the school's website but something that needs to be embedded in the very culture of a school. And as management guru Peter Drucker reportedly said: 'Culture eats strategy for breakfast.'

It works by building relationships (and you have to work hard at relationships, particularly when the relationships are hard). If you improve relationships then, for the schools I've worked with, this has meant increased attendance, dramatically lowered exclusion rates and increased engagement in learning, which has in turn led to higher attainment. On top of that it teaches those who run schools, and who are run by schools, to build a sense of community, to spend time developing social capital and to transform engagement with all stakeholders. And it serves as an antidote to hypocrisy.

There are some simple ways of doing this: a smile or a 'Good morning, how was your weekend?' are a good start. Then there's using restorative circles to build connections more formally to enhance relationships and to increase participation, influence and voice across the school community. One example would be to do a 'check-in circle' on a Monday and 'check-out circle' on a Friday – you could use tutor time for this. And, remember, it's not just rearranging the chairs that makes these processes so powerful – it's the way that we share the voice and the power.

Other quick wins include using affective statements and language outside of conflict and tensions to reinforce the positive side of relationship building. What if all staff gave 10 pieces of positive feedback to 10 different children each day? What impact would this have on the school community? We spend too much time catching people out making the wrong choices rather than catching them in doing the right thing. After all, my experience tells me that when you focus on problems, you end up with more problems. When you focus on possibilities, you'll have more opportunities.

By investing in restorative practice, schools can be less reactive – spending time putting measures in place for when it all kicks off and dealing with the emotional fall-out when it does

– and more proactive – helping to avoid the situations when it might kick off in the first place. How much time each week do you currently spend reacting, and how much time do you spend planning ahead to get it right in the first place?

So, first things first. The idea that we can separate the academic achievement of our children from their social development amazes me. We can't. Children are what they are. Agreed, poor behaviour cannot be an excuse for underachieving academically. But nor should a focus on academic achievement be done without understanding and embracing the role a school plays in the social and emotional development of its children.

Every child is different and they all have the right to expect from you the conditions necessary for growth if they are to feel safe, well-connected and have a true sense of belonging. In this environment they are able to take risks, ask quality questions, feel free to make mistakes and explore new ideas. However, this cannot be achieved when a school is led by an over-controlling, authoritarian system based on rules, blame and sanctions. Such institutions are often shored up by deeply held notions about power and control that promote the need to make things unpleasant for someone when they have done something wrong or 'misbehaved'. (Of course, the culture of naming and shaming, blame and punishment is foisted on schools themselves by those in power in the name of 'standards'. Laugh, cry or fume?)

Restorative practice takes a different stance. It is a way of dealing with conflict and tensions that acts to rebuild relationships, not make them worse. It creates a common language and a common approach for fostering a sense of social responsibility and shared accountability for the whole community.

The golden rule? Separate the behaviour from the person, the deed from the doer and the act from the actor.

To achieve these broader outcomes, restorative practice proposes an explicit framework through which relationships are built, maintained and repaired with the specific aim of fostering an environment in which children are capable of being truly engaged in their learning.

But this requires a shift away from punitive practice to a more relational culture, and this is what many schools find hard – not helped by the current predilection for direct transmission of facts from the front matched by draconian measures to subdue bored children!

Instead, a relational approach focuses on building a strong values based culture in schools that fosters belonging over exclusion, social engagement over control and meaningful accountability over punishment. After all, punishment alone, although effective as a weapon of control, simply creates resentment rather than reflection, change or growth. You'd think schools didn't want children to learn to think for themselves!

Traditionally, when a child does something wrong, the questions that are asked are along the lines of 'Who's to blame?', 'What rule has been broken?', 'How are we going to punish them?' This way of thinking and working is very adversarial, where punishment is used *pour encourager les autres* and where those who are affected are often ignored. What's more, it means we spend far too much time on the problem and not enough time on the solution; too much time in the past and not enough time in the future. And you can't change the past.

Restorative practice is an approach that involves both the wrongdoer and the harmed person. It even involves, when appropriate, other members of the school community. The purpose of bringing together these players is to find a solution to the perceived problem or issue. It is solution focused. It involves dialogue. It is more about asking questions than doling out answers. It asks a different set of questions: 'What has happened?', 'Who has been affected and how?', 'How can we make things better?', 'What can we learn from this experience?'

By asking more and better questions, rather than always handing down answers, we encourage a climate of possibility, of choice, of growth; one where the players can gain trust, take risks and grow in confidence. It is in this climate – one of safe, respectful, boundaried conversations – that we can start to give vulnerable people back their power and help them find their authentic voice.

When we help students to reflect more, and we ask thinking and feeling questions, we create better links between thoughts, emotions and actions. This in turn increases connectedness, kindness and emotional intelligence. It leads to an increase in positive emotions and also encourages the appropriate expression of these emotions. If you express it, you feel it and if you feel it, you're more likely to move on. By taking this approach we have a genuine opportunity to decrease conflicts and disruptions and genuinely encourage forgiveness.

Of course, none of this happens overnight. We must support staff in meaningful ways – staff we have identified as struggling in their relationships with young people. Absolutely central to our children's progress is the behaviour of the adults around them. The biggest influence on a child is the role modelling of adults. But if you aren't modelling what you're teaching, you're teaching something different. The quality of dialogue, discussion and focus displayed by all adults needs to shift from blame to understanding. All teachers should be encouraged to solve more issues themselves, taking ownership and responsibility rather than escalating problems and the punishments and sanctions that go with them. Young people in turn are encouraged to become increasingly self-regulating and develop as confident problem-solvers, with positive spin-offs in their learning at school and beyond.

It's a magical process to witness and transformative in ways that you wouldn't believe. Yet it's not magic. So much of it is simply common sense. It needs a major shift in mindset for any school where doing things *to* children and not *with* them seems built into its culture. It's a big change but it can be done. And it's a change that starts the minute you stop screaming at that child, look at the values on the wall and let your actions scream at them instead.

Recommended book:

John Kotter and Holger Rathgeber, *Our Iceberg Is Melting: Changing and Succeeding Under Any Conditions* (London: Macmillan, 2006)

Chapter 25

If Coaching Is the Answer – What Is the Question?

How Professional Development Is All In the Mind

Jackie Beere OBE

How can we make the performance management process in our school more effective?

Is performance management the powerhouse that drives professional development for each and every teacher and member of staff in our school?

Are continuing professional development (CPD) and performance management making a measurable difference to the quality of teaching?

Do we have the evidence for progress in quality of teaching?

Have we measured the impact of our CPD on our results and outcomes for pupils?

Do any of these questions keep you awake at night?

Staff development in schools has moved a long way from having generic INSET days and the odd external course for the lucky ones. School self-evaluation and the tracking of pupil outcomes have evolved and led the best schools to create a self-reflective learning culture. They link school development priorities to training programmes that include optional twilight sessions, learning forums, research awards and focused peer lesson observation. Appraisal as a paper exercise that lists some ambitious targets pulled out of Fischer Family Trust data, and which gets dusted off once a year for the compulsory chat with your line manager in daytime training, has long gone – hasn't it?

I'm not sure that all schools have quite discovered the secret of creating a culture where *all* teachers and support staff, new and old, ambitious and time serving, passionate and cynical, believe they are on a continuous learning journey. A journey in which they all continually assess their impact and improve their effectiveness so that 'best practice is identified, modelled and shared'.[1]

Out there in the virtual world, there is a huge community of teachers who tweet and blog and share their opinions and ideas about what works (and what doesn't) in their classrooms. Flicking through the *TES* on a Sunday morning or reading a worthy educational tome in the holidays is now being replaced by quick fire, real life answers to questions like, 'How can I motivate my bright but coasting Year 10 girls/Year 4 boys?' or 'Does anyone out there have any resources for delivering literacy skills within science?' The ideas, links, stories and comments that bounce back can be both thought provoking and downright useful. Online communities such as TES Connect also have a huge number of lesson plans, resources and articles that are easy to access and include forums to join.

It's addictive to become part of this online community of teachers passionate about learning and how it works – teachers willing to learn, share their resources and try out new methods. Unfortunately, in my experience as a trainer, I see only a minority of teachers with either the time or inclination to use this valuable developmental resource. When I ask the question at training events, 'How many of you use Twitter as a CPD tool?', usually only a couple of hands go up.

Although we would love to think that every teacher has become an active self-improver, endlessly curious about how to move their practice forward and able to use the latest technology to do so, I think we have some way to go before this is embedded as part of professional development for all teachers. Some staff will never want to take this route to self-improvement, and some teachers think they are already doing enough. But leaders are now even more responsible and accountable for the development and continuous improvement of all staff. So how can we help more teachers to be motivated to improve so that performance management works?

Shaun Allison, in his excellent book *Perfect Teacher-Led CPD*, makes the point that most teachers plateau after two or three years and begin to stick to what they have found works, rather than continually refining and evolving their skills, as the very best teachers do.[2] He suggests offering a wide range of continuing professional development that is both bespoke for individuals and congruent with school priorities. The best INSET days should offer activities that drive forward the vision and tie together our mutual objectives, but in addition offer a choice of optional development activities for teachers and other staff. These could include research forums, peer observation, subject-based training or community TeachMeets – teacher-led events where best (and worst) practice is shared, stored online or transmitted electronically to share with colleagues. The best INSET will also include mentoring for new or needy teachers with set targets for improvement. Everyone will keep a CPD portfolio showing how they are addressing and progressing towards their personal goals for becoming a better teacher. All these strategies will create a culture in which teachers know that standing still is not an option and that becoming a great teacher is not a destination but a journey that never ends.

However, the evidence shows that the secret to being the very best teacher you can be is not so much about what you *do*, it is about how you *think*. In my research for *The Practically Perfect Teacher*, I found that the evidence has shown again and again that it is the mindset of the teacher that is the key to, and the most powerful indicator of, their effectiveness.[3] No matter how good our CPD offer is, or how high our expectations and targets for teachers are, if we want sustainable, consistently great schools where all teachers continually improve themselves and their students, it is teachers' mindsets we need to work on.

But what can we do to create the growth mindset that Carol Dweck cites as the key to success in her work[4] – the same growth mindset that chimes perfectly with John Hattie's extensive research outcomes which show that school leaders and teachers need to be 'agents of change'?[5] Teachers need to enjoy the challenge of change, avoid making excuses or simply 'do their best' and realise that outcomes for children are a result of *their* teaching.

Teaching has never been harder than it is now, and that is unlikely to change. However, everything else is! New Ofsted frameworks always seem to be looming. New government administrations continuously move the goalposts with brand new initiatives to implement. Our assessment and exam system is in a state of flux, and it will evolve with the intention of making it harder for schools and teachers to 'play the system'. We are already seeing single exam entries, less coursework, reduced vocational course accreditation and Progress 8 measures to assess how much progress *all* children make.

Big change, high stress and huge demands on our time and energy as teachers and school leaders are not going to go away. To cope with this we need to create a culture that adapts to change and relentlessly creates a staff mindset of growth and development. The best way to do this is through developing a coaching culture. Not coaching for those that are 'in need of extra support' but coaching for *everyone* to:

+ Develop the ability to ask coaching questions that tease ideas out from the coachee and help them move forward with their thinking.

+ Tweak their practice to move forward in small steps as part of their continuous learning journey.

+ Commit to trying something new that they have thought of, committed to and considered how it will be evaluated.

+ Keep a written record of the decision and how its outcome/impact will be measured.

◆   Follow up by evaluating the outcome with peer lesson observations, work scrutiny, pupil interviews, etc. that both coach and coachee learn from and keep a record of.

What's more, the aim eventually would be to use coaching questions and a coaching model in the classroom so that teachers can coach children in developing the right sort of mindset, and also so that children can learn to coach each other.[6]

So, where do you start? Here are seven steps you can take to get the coaching ball rolling:

1. Train all staff in the benefits of having a growth mindset that focuses on effort as the path to mastery, and that challenge and mistakes are simply part of the learning experience.

2. Establish the fact that all teachers are on a learning journey – one which never ends but evolves – and that reflecting on and adjusting your practice regularly is an essential part of this journey.

3. Establish coaching as part of the journey where someone else challenges you to evolve your practice. Embed it as part of 'the way we do things round here' and make it an integral part of the CPD system of the school. If the coachee wishes, coaching records can be kept in CPD portfolios as evidence and used in performance management; otherwise, the process remains confidential to the coachee and coach.

4. Begin by training coaches that are already keen learners and influencers but not necessarily line managers. Pair them up with members of staff for their regular coaching sessions. As more staff become familiar with the power of coaching, new pairings can develop and evolve. Use a coaching evaluation system to check what is working well.

5. Encourage the use of social media and informal staffroom conversations about learning by having a shared learning board or magazine (real or virtual) that displays

ideas, articles, blogs, case studies etc. to exemplify a shared, relentless curiosity about learning.

6. Establish various research groups which evaluate the buy-in and impact of all the CPD and performance management strategies used in the school to ensure they are contributing to improved teaching and learning outcomes.

7. Get the research groups and all staff to constantly reflect and ask the following question, often: does what we do to help you become a better teacher really work? What can we do to help you learn more about what works?

And as Jim Collins says in his fascinating book, *Good to Great*, the very best leaders, those who take their school to 'outstanding', will face the brutal facts and make sure that they get the right people on the bus in the right places.[7] Any teacher who says 'I can't change' or 'I don't really need to learn anything else – I'm there', will be dropped off at the next bus stop.

Recommended book:

Carol Dweck, *Mindset: The Psychology of Success* (New York: Random House, 2006)

Notes

1 Ofsted, School Inspection Handbook (January 2015). Ref: 120101. Available at: https://www.gov.uk/government/uploads/system/uploads/attachment_data/file/391531/School_inspection_handbook.pdf, p. 46.
2 S. Allison, *Perfect Teacher-Led CPD* (Carmarthen: Independent Thinking Press, 2014).
3 J. Beere, *The Practically Perfect Teacher* (Carmarthen: Independent Thinking Press, 2014).
4 C. Dweck, *Mindset: The Psychology of Success* (New York: Random House, 2006).
5 J. Hattie, *Visible Learning For Teachers: Maximizing Impact on Learning* (New York and London: Routledge, 2012).

6   The iSTRIDE model from *The Practically Perfect Teacher* (pp. 57–58), which is based on Will Thomas' work, is as good a place to start as any when it comes to an easy-to-use coaching system.

7   J. Collins, *Good to Great* (London: Random House, 2001).

Chapter 26

The Future Classroom Today

The Five Pillars of Digital Learning

Simon Pridham

By 2016 every single pupil in our global education systems will have been born in the 21st century, whilst all our teachers will be from the 20th century. This single fact alone should be a wake-up call for our education leaders worldwide. But what exactly is the relevance of this startling fact, and does it change the dynamics and characteristics of a 3-year-old taking their first steps into the world of education today? Undoubtedly, yes!

The 21st century learner now enters our classrooms as a different specimen to what they were just five years ago. These pupils, using technology, peer support, networks of collaboration and mobile online resources, are at complete ease when building an education *for themselves* anywhere and at anytime. A decade ago, outside the classroom walls, information for your average 11-year-old was scarce. In 2015, information can be found in abundance: Google, YouTube, online blogs, hangouts, social media, the list goes on and on. Therefore, pupils need to see their teachers as modellers of learning, master learners, risk-takers, facilitators, collaborators and creators, and to top it off those teachers have to be tech-savvy. We have to change as educators and, as a profession, we should be excited by that.

The 21st century classroom, where technology is as accessible as paper and pen, allows you to personalise the learning like never before in order to develop independent and creative thinkers. It also allows your pupils to drive their educational journey as co-pilots with you rather than as passengers. And, as a former primary head teacher, I am including our youngest pupils in this too. The alternative is to continue with the status quo and to further entrench the notion that schools are a parallel universe to the society outside the school gates.

However, we have to remember that without the brilliance of the teacher spotting *the right opportunity in the right context* within our classrooms, this magic never materialises. Over the last five years or so, I have worked with pupils, teachers, schools, local authorities and governments in offering strategic as well as practical advice when trying to bridge the generational gap between pupils and teachers, using new technologies to do so. The commonality about all the successful programmes I've seen is that to embrace technologies effectively across your school community you need to consider five key pillars.

1. **An agreed whole school community vision and plan**

    What is your vision for using technology, and how will this be communicated effectively to the wider community? Parental involvement in this process is vital as they will need to understand why this is important, what their role is and how this is a massive opportunity for them as a parent and as a lifelong learner.

2. **The construction of a school digital team**

    There is one very important point to stress at the outset: *a school's ICT coordinator is not the person to lead the school on their digital journey*. They have a role to play in the digital team, but the e-learning manager should be the person who takes the lead. Important features of the e-learning manager's job include responsibility for current and emerging technologies to impact across the entire school community, the management of the pupil digital leaders as well as lead teachers and assistants who can support the school's vision, and communicating this strategy to the wider community. The digital team should look something like this:

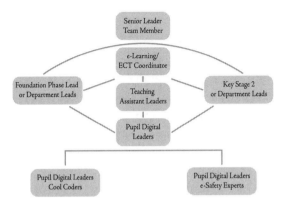

A. N. Example School – Digital Team Structure.

3. **Technology and teaching and learning goals linked to the school improvement plan**

The life of a teacher is most certainly a busy one. As a past executive head teacher, I know from personal experience that if you add to teachers' ever increasing workload then you are in danger of not being able to convert your vision into working practice. That's why it is vitally important to use the school's existing or future development plan priorities *alongside* your digital aims.

4. **The whole team needs an investment of time and effort**

Managers and leaders take time to develop expertise, and this is no different with a digital team. All members must receive the appropriate mentoring, be given the necessary time to develop within their role and also be able to evaluate impact and effectiveness against set criteria.

5.   Strive for community cohesion

As true community hubs, schools have incredible opportunities to engage with parents, intergenerational learners and wider community groups using technology. The pupil digital leaders can build relationships with community members through sharing skills and passing on digital knowledge, and the school and its resources can be used as the focus point. This also allows the wider community to contribute and give something back to the school in a positive way, such as sharing their skills with children or helping the school in the many areas in which they have expertise.

These five pillars are built on the assumption that the school also has robust Wi-Fi and an agreed infrastructure to enable aspirations to be realised. Sadly, schools are amongst the final public bastions where Wi-Fi is a privilege rather than an essential ingredient. This in itself brings problems, with some schools making the investment a key priority and others not. This in turn means that 21st century teaching and learning is not equitable from school to school. This has to change.

It's widely accepted that Key Stage 3 pupils have access to more information through their smartphones today than I did in my entire university library as a student. Yet, a high percentage of secondary educators still ban pupils using smartphones in their classrooms. Talk about missing a trick, alienating a generation and turning pupils off school! What society needs now are people who can ask good questions, come up with creative solutions, critically examine those possibilities, work out which solution is most likely to be effective and then communicate their ideas effectively enough to motivate others to action. As far back as the 1900s that wise old owl Albert Einstein said: 'Education is not the learning of facts, but the training of the mind to think.'

To conclude, learning institutions that are thriving in the 21st century have classrooms that embrace the social, physical and emotional aspects of learning. Always remember that technology is simply one part of this environment. A creative curriculum, highly effective pedagogy and mobile technology together create the surroundings where pupils, like my daughter who is 4, feel valued and challenged. We need to realise that some of the best teachers my daughter will ever experience will be virtual or online and sitting the other side of the world. This is a cultural mind shift that we, as educators, have to accept and embrace.

Prepare yourself for the 21st century learner who is now entering your school, folks – they are here!

Recommended book:

Guy Claxton, *What's the Point of School? Rediscovering the Heart of Education* (Oxford: Oneworld Publications, 2008)

Chapter 27

The Monkey's Nuts

Creating a Challenging Curriculum

Jonathan Lear

If we take the risk out of education, there is a real chance that we take out the education altogether.

Gert J. J. Biesta

I had it all planned. I'd recorded it the day before because I knew it would be exactly the kind of thing that my 7-year-old daughter would be interested in. She'd been learning about the rainforest at school and as soon as I saw the title, *Wild Brazil*, I knew I was on to a winner. Sixty minutes of educational 'dad time'. With her younger sister in tow, we sat down to watch. It was probably about three minutes in when things started to go wrong. Out of nowhere, and with absolutely no warning, we were faced with the most gratuitous monkey sex that I've ever seen.

I was expecting the monkeys. They had been mentioned in the synopsis. What they omitted to mention was the sex. It turned out that the entire documentary was about the capuchin monkey mating season, and along with being highly intelligent, this particular troupe of monkeys were pretty voracious in the bedroom department. It wasn't long before their admittedly impressive antics drew some uncomfortable questions from my two young viewers. Like any self-respecting dad, I lied about what was unfolding on the screen and set about coming up with multiple excuses about what was happening. I decided that this was my only option given the fact that they wouldn't let me turn it off, and to be fair, in-between the bursts of monkey porn, there were some great little nuggets of information about the Amazon.

Forty-five minutes in, the mating season was finished and the documentary seemed to be coming to an end. Whilst the monkeys had a well-deserved post-coital rest, the documentary makers had put together one of those 'behind the scenes, this is how we filmed it' kind of sections, and within this was a moment that made watching the entire show worthwhile.

Interested in just how intelligent capuchin monkeys actually are, the scientists decided to set them a test by creating a monkey-proof box. Inside the box was the monkeys' favourite snack – nuts – and to get at them, they had to press a lever on the front that released the nuts from a chute. Now, capuchin monkeys were clever. They could use tools like sticks and rocks, but they'd never seen or used a lever before. With the box primed and ready, the scientists backed off to a safe distance and watched.

At first, what seemed like the whole troupe descended from the trees. The box was new and interesting and the monkeys wanted a look. Before long, they were attempting their tried-and-tested techniques for getting most monkey jobs done. They sniffed, licked, nibbled, poked and then smashed at the box with rocks. Nothing happened. After a while, they gave up and drifted back into the forest.

Whilst all this was happening, one member of the troupe had been sitting to one side just watching. When the others had gone, he got up and went over to the box. After a few sniffs and a bit of a poke, he climbed down in front of it and looked at the lever. With his head cocked to one side, he reached out with his paw, placed it on the lever and pressed. Immediately, the nuts tumbled down the chute. He couldn't believe his luck, and after a quick check to see no one was looking, he ate them, and then pressed the lever again and again, each time getting more and more nuts. When he'd had enough he toddled off into the trees and emerged a few seconds later with a friend. After bringing him over to the box, he showed him how it worked, and after the excitement died down, the friend was also at it with the lever, stuffing his face with nuts. Along with the entertainment factor that goes hand in hand with any animal-related problem-solving activity, what really stood out was the way that the scientists summed up the success of this particular troupe of monkeys. They described them as having 'insatiable curiosity and the ability to learn from each other'.

As a teacher, this phrase struck me instantly, and hearing it made me think about my own little monkeys, sitting either side of me on the sofa, still trying to comprehend exactly what it was their dad was making them watch. They are both insatiably curious, but then most young people are.

In foundation stage, our youngest children experience the monkey-proof box on a daily basis, but then as they get older, and as learning becomes more formal, we ditch the monkey-proofing for the path of least resistance – the clearest route from A to B – and their curiosity and creative thinking begin to fade.

But what if it didn't? What if we kept hold of some of that monkey-ness? The scientists didn't teach the monkeys to be curious or to think creatively, they just created the right conditions to draw it out. They could have just taken the nuts, put them on a plate and left it in the clearing. The monkeys would have rolled up, eaten the nuts and then clambered off home again. The outcome in both cases would have been the same – but thanks to the monkey-proof box, the journey to get there was harder and the monkeys were pushed to test their curiosity and apply their creative thinking.

The box inspired curiosity because it was unusual, different and new. The challenge had purpose because it was real, and the process of learning was challenging, awkward, difficult but ultimately rewarding. If you think about it, the curriculum we're faced with is nuts on a plate. But if we really want our young people to become the insatiably curious creative thinkers of tomorrow, we need to break free from the comfort of straightforwardness and embrace the risk and challenge of the monkey-proof box.

Recommended book:

Gert J. J. Biesta, *The Beautiful Risk of Education* (Boulder, CO: Paradigm, 2013)

Chapter 28

Now Can You See What I'm Thinking?

Schools, Behaviour and Art Therapy

Bethan Stracy-Burbridge

It is well-known that school provides a social education as well as an academic one. If it were not so, our children could quite satisfactorily remain at home teaching themselves. Learning how to fit in with others is as much a process of learning about yourself as it is learning about others, and as schools and society ramp up the pressure on ever younger children such learning is vital to ensure that we grow up physically and mentally well. However, children often lack the range of verbal vocabulary to express themselves, especially when the topic is their inner emotional turmoil. This is where art therapists have a powerful and proven role to play.

In brief, our role when working within education (we work in a wide variety of settings) is to help young people identify new strategies, thoughts and behaviours that will enhance their physiological and emotional well-being. This is even more valuable when we are working with young people who are growing up in very challenging environments or who have gone through any one of a range of particularly stressful and potentially damaging experiences. Using what we could call a systemic approach (i.e. we're not about sticking plasters), and with the assistance of parents and teachers willing to make positive changes, art therapists are able to help build that all-important emotional resilience in children.

Before we get to work, though, there are two important areas to get right. The first is to acknowledge that we do not interact with children in a vacuum. In other words, our environment plays a large role in shaping who we are. For example, whenever we are in a group situation, our own particular experience of family dynamics will have a part to play in how we act and react in all our interactions with other members of the group. Within an education setting, we can make both *vertical* (relating to a parental figure) and *horizontal* (siblings) attachments with those around us.[1] These engagements, for better or for worse, are determined by our previous life experiences. It is important to be aware, as teachers, that we often assume 'parental' position, albeit subconsciously. Yalom describes how the group facilitator should acknowledge the difficulties that can occur when wearing multiple hats concurrently.[2] In other words, for teachers, the dual role of being both the disciplinarian and the supporter can be a difficult road to travel.

The second area to address when it comes to laying the groundwork for any successful art therapy intervention is good communication. This is something that is best addressed at the beginning of the relationship. It is here that you set down the ground rules of what is expected from each party, which helps avoid stress and confusion as the process unfolds. For example, Rumbold observes that 'some team members will want to know the group rules before exposing their beliefs'.[3] In other words, it is important to make the child feel safe and valued before a successful relationship can be formed. What's more, 'mutual communication tends to be pointed towards solving a problem rather than towards attacking a person or group'.[4] The word 'mutual' is important here. Communication involves all members of the intervention community (for example, some children are better talkers than listeners and seem capable of having a conversation with themselves in the hope that others will join in – a bit like Twitter). What's more, as Rogers highlights, it is vital that all communication is solution focused.

Communicating can take many forms, and with art therapy we are particularly interested in what cannot be verbalised but may be represented in other ways, especially the visual. For example, an inner struggle a child may be experiencing may manifest itself by way of a chair being thrown across the room in the middle of a lesson. This 'visual' image is a form of communication through action, perhaps stemming from anxiety or fear, and results in aggression and confusion. Staff members can be quick to use the term 'problem behaviour' to describe those children who disrupt the flow of learning in schools. While this behaviour often results in interruptions for the teacher and the class, it is often the only 'solution' that the child can come up with at that time. This 'visual image through action' creates a physical, visual and real manifestation of their inner problem and gains the child attention from the adult. It is, therefore, a form of communication.

Evidence from multiple sources indicates that when a stimulus in the present overlaps with a memory of a past stressful or traumatic event, the likelihood of triggering an emotive response is increased.[5] Had you known that the same student who had thrown the chair in class had witnessed domestic violence before the age of 2, would you have reacted differently to their actions? Which approach would you use in this situation – immediate punishment or understanding their story? And how might either provoke positive change in the student?

So, as staff members, it is important to recognise that 'poor behaviour' can be a form of 'communication through action' and that it is a form of communication that needs to be heard. So, the question starts to shift from 'How do we prevent this action?' to 'How do we understand the action?' If we simply ask the former, we may achieve our goal by actually making things worse for the child. By asking the latter, we achieve our goal and, in the process, improve the overall emotional well-being of the child. Where art therapy comes in is that, rather than the 'visual image through action' being destructive and dangerous, it becomes a form of art. We, the adults, build a bridge into their world, rather than expecting the children to always adhere to the rules of ours.

The art therapist, then, steps in and invites the child to express themselves safely (for them and for others) through art, giving that child the freedom to explore and experiment and to experience being in control of substances such as clay, paint and cardboard. These creations regularly hold emotional content, similar to that of a transitional object; that is to say, one that provides some sort of psychological comfort, such as a security blanket, plugging the gap between mother and child or therapist and the child's personal reflective space.[6] Once we have identified the need for communication and helped give it some form of safe expression, we can then proceed to support the child's understanding of their 'visual voice'.

Sometimes we forget how scary it can be to experience change through a child's eyes, especially if their inner world is already unsettled and destabilised. I often support groups of identified students whose only stability is their educational environment. This becomes a huge source of negative stress when they are about to make the transition from primary to secondary, for example, or are an older student about to fly the educational nest, their future uncertain and foggy. Offering a reflective space where art therapy directives, such as 'build a desert island as a team', serve to reinforce group cohesion can help to bolster inter- and intra-personal skills and the confidence they will need to transition to the next stage of their lives. Their worries have been voiced and that voice has been heard. At a more clinical level (and done only with expert support), offering a space in which children can regress to an earlier developmental stage, a stage where a particular trauma was experienced, can serve to address unhelpful behaviours that are present as a result of that trauma and transform them into more helpful coping strategies. It is a process that can be quite magical!

Within the field of neuroscience, we are now able to see the effects that a particular sort of childhood has on the developing brain of a child and the way in which the brain of an un-loved child can grow in a very different way from one who is nourished emotionally. We also know that high levels of unmitigated stress as a child can lead to an unhelpful intolerance of stress as adults, as if our 'stress thermostat' has been set to high as a result of our early experiences. Therefore, it is reasonable to suggest that every interaction we have with a student (good, bad and somewhere in-between), changes not only the child but also, as the brain remains plastic throughout its life, us as teachers and adults. It's as if you were given a ball of clay to hold – your imprints would be visible to those who looked hard enough. You shape the students you meet every day, just as they shape you. What art therapy does is to ensure that process is a positive one for all concerned.

Recommended book:

Andrew Curran, *The Little Book of Big Stuff About the Brain* (Carmarthen: Independent Thinking Press, 2008)

Notes

1   H. Geddes, *Attachment in the Classroom: The Links Between Children's Early Experience, Emotional Well-Being and Performance In School* (London: Worth Publishing, 2006).

2   I. D. Yalom, *The Theory and Practice of Group Psychotherapy* (New York: Basic Books, 1975).

3   J. Rumbold, *Knowing Differently: Arts-Based and Collaborative Research Methods* (New York: Nova Science Publishers, 2008), p. 288.

4   N. Rogers, *The Creative Connection for Groups: Person-Centered Expressive Arts For Healing and Social Change* (Palo Alto, CA: Science and Behavior Books, 2011), p. 336.

5   See B. A. van der Kolk, *Psychological Trauma* (Washington, DC: American Psychiatric Press, 1987); I. L. McCann and L. A. Pearlman, Vicarious traumatization: A framework for understanding the psychological effects of working with victims, *Journal of Traumatic Stress* 3(1), (1990): 131–149; J. L. Herman, *Trauma and Recovery: The Aftermath of Violence* (New York: Basic Books, 1992); H. Lubin and D. R. Johnson, *Trauma-Centered Group Psychotherapy for Women: A Clinician's Manual* (New York, Taylor & Francis, 2008).

6   D. W. Winnicott, Transitional Objects and Transitional Phenomena (1951), in D. W. Winnicott, *Collected Papers: Through Paediatrics to Psychoanalysis* (London: Tavistock, 1958), pp. 229–242.

Chapter 29

The Aesthetic Moment

When What We Learn and How We Feel Turn Out To Be the Same Thing

Martin Illingworth

Here's an idea. Next time your students are reading a book, let them read the book. Next time they are playing netball, let them play netball. Next time they are listening to Mozart, shut up and let them do just that. Learning is more lovable when it is being done for its own sake; right here, right now. When the learning is valuable in itself, then your students will see the point.

However, if we want to really destroy children's love of books, netball, Mozart and everything else that can make life wonderful, then let's all carry on with the current penchant for 20-minute progress checking, tedious data, box-ticking assessment for learning, pointless tyrannical writing, unreasonable accountability, exam hoop-jumping, Ofsted panic and brutally humiliating pressure.

I got lucky during one Ofsted. I'd already been 'seen' and had relaxed (schoolboy error), thinking that I wouldn't be 'seen' again. Then, in walks the inspector just as my A level English literature group and I are reading the bit in Sebastian Faulks' *Birdsong* where the granddaughter visits the memorial in Thiepval to the missing soldiers at the Battle of the Somme. As a group, we had just come back from a trip to the battlefields and memorials of Belgium and northern France. We had been to Thiepval. What this means is that we have shared the moment that the granddaughter is going through (staggered by the loss of life in the First World War) and it is important to us because it has been part of our 'real' lives as well as the artificial life of the classroom.

As my (our?) judge and jury crosses the threshold, I am saying to Amy (because she cried for about an hour on the spot the granddaughter is on in the novel), ' ... and you know how that feels, Amy.'

And Amy does know exactly how 'that' feels, and so does the whole group because the experience holds us together and gives us a commonality that is of our own making. We know how Amy feels and we are spending time unpacking that feeling. It is raw as hell and full of wonder and we are awed by the enormity of it all, the pain of it all and the amazement at how it can hurt still – nearly a hundred years later.

As my old head teacher would have said, 'Awe and wonder, Martin, awe and wonder.'

Afterwards, the Ofsted inspector told me, 'You could have cut the air with a knife,' and that was, to be fair, exactly what she was looking for. And I know what she means ...

She was referring to what I call 'the aesthetic moment'. The moment when you and your group are in the instant. You are not practising for next week's test. You are not revising for next year's exam. You are not doing things to prepare young people for their future. What you are investigating is all about right here, right now, and you are doing it because it matters. Deeply.

And so it goes; the art connects with the lives of the students. The room we sit in is made irrelevant because we are transfixed by the thought of the missing. We are remembering the search for our own surnames on those memorial stones and then, weeks later, looking on the Commonwealth War Graves Commission website, researching the lives of our extended families. A connection is made with the missing and those young minds developing in my care. The young are in touch with their cultures, their history, their identity.

I had told the parents, sitting anxiously at the meeting to explain the visit to the battle-grounds, that I would bring their children back as different people. I have succeeded in this. And when we return from our journey, there is a quiet drift away from the coach to the cars and arms of parents; a sober seriousness, a need to tell what they have seen.

And do you think my students could write about the novel when it came to exam time? Absolutely they could. And why? Because it was part of them. Our journey to the graves, our individual research into our families' involvement, the transcripts we had collected from the war, the film we watched at the local cinema and the presentations we gave around how we felt. Not what we had 'learnt' but how we felt. There's a difference of intent. But, curiously, when you start with feeling, then think about learning, you realise that what we learn and how we feel can turn out to be the same thing.

And in truth, I haven't really 'taught' them anything at all. No lectures from the front (excuse the pun). No expert knowledge about the war. Instead, I have stood beside them, shaking my head too at the incomprehensible. But these students believe in me because I care; I care about the topic and I care about them. That, I suspect, is expertise enough in their eyes. We have investigated. We haven't been told, we've been shown. We have made our own minds up. We have made meaning (if, indeed, meaning can be made from this madness). From the First World War my students have found what I call 'new' knowledge.

They chose what and when to write things down, and we looked at the needs of the exam about a month beforehand. But by then it was a foregone conclusion; my students were 'experts' bursting to share what they knew.

And, on reflection, I couldn't and didn't care less what the inspector thought about our lesson. Whether your lesson is any good or not is in the children's eyes, not on the inspector's clipboard. We were busy, we were thoughtful and we were engaged in matters far more pressing than demonstrating that learning was going on in the classroom and progress was being made. We needed to see what happened next as the granddaughter lifts herself up from the steps at Thiepval. She is troubled by the past. It has unsettled her. She needs to think things through. And we are with her every step of the way. Truly great literature has connected to the real lives of the readers in my classroom.

Teachers often say they don't have time. Maybe they're right. In lessons such as the ones I am describing here there is no time. No time to worry about inspectors. No time to worry about whether we are making progress. (It will stop us from making progress.) No time to worry about making sure you never use 'And' at the beginning of a sentence. And no time to worry about the noisy clamour from on high that beats at the door! The door is shut. We will do what we want and there is only now, this aesthetic moment.

Recommended book:

R. J. Stewart, *Clap Your Hands For Daddy* (N.p.: RJS Press, 2014)

To find out more and keep up to date with our work at Independent Thinking please visit www.independentthinking.com

978-190442438-3

978-178135055-3

www.independentthinkingpress.com